The Invisible Farmers

The Invisible Farmers

Women in Agricultural Production

Carolyn E. Sachs

ROWMAN & ALLANHELD
Totowa, New Jersey

ROWMAN & ALLANHELD

Published in the United States of America in 1983
by Rowman & Allanheld
(A division of Littlefield, Adams & Company)
81 Adams Drive, Totowa, New Jersey 07512

Library of Congress Cataloging in Publication Data

Sachs, Carolyn E., 1950–
    The invisible farmers.

    Bibliography: p.
    Includes index.
    1. Women farmers—United States—History.   2. Women
farmers—United States.   I. Title.
S441.S25 1983   305.4′33′0973   82-22824
ISBN 0-86598-094-2

84 85/ 10 9 8 7 6 5 4 3 2
Printed in the United States of America

Contents

Tables and Figures

Tables

Figures

Acknowledgments

This work evolved from discussions with women farmers. The willingness of these women to give their time and to share their experiences made this book possible, and I am grateful to all of them.

Many other persons provided assistance and support. During the process of writing, Lawrence Busch provided much needed criticism and encouragement. In addition, Janet Bokemeier, Dwight Billings, and Herbert Reid read several drafts and offered many helpful suggestions. Although it is not possible to list everyone who has in one way or another supported me through this process, I do want to express my appreciation to Beverly Tuite, Anne Flynn, Sally Maggard, Randi Randolph, Pam Woods, Virginia Caye, Virginia Sachs, Judy Sachs, John Sachs, Cindy Olivas, and Janice Taylor.

My appreciation is extended to the many people who have done research in the area of women in agriculture. I only wish I had encountered the many supportive and committed people prior to writing the book. I would like to thank the following people for their willingness to share their insights and for their continuing interest in farm women: Sarah Elbert, Christina Gladwin, Cornelia Flora, Laura Raynolds, Susan Abbott, Irene Tinker, Alice Anderson, Rachel Rosenfeld, Joan Jensen, Gould Colman, and Eugene Wilkening.

I would also like to thank for their assistance in typing drafts of the manuscript Carol Grove, Barbara Sachs, Ann Flynn, and especially Linnea Noll for her enthusiasm in the typing of the final manuscript. Finally I would like to thank my publishers for their support.

An earlier version of this book was written as a doctoral dissertation in the Department of Sociology at the University of Kentucky.

Introduction

As this book will demonstrate, women have participated in agricultural production throughout the history of the United States. As a consequence of a powerful sexual division of labor, however, women have often been restricted to domestic work and so their participation has been consistently overlooked and undervalued. There is still a strong tendency to see men as farmers and women as farmer's wives.

The primary purpose of this book is to explore the full nature of women's involvement in agricultural production through the use of historical research and interviews with contemporary farm women. The historical evidence demonstrates that women have been involved in agriculture, while the interviews reveal their continued presence in farm work. A second goal of this work is to show why these facts are so often overlooked and to alleviate the uneven sexual division of labor by offering practical suggestions for reform.

Understanding the position of women on farms requires an understanding both of the economic forces operating upon the structure of agriculture in particular and of the position of women in society at large. While transformations in the structure of agriculture affect both women and men, this study focuses on those changes that have particular impact upon women. Of equal importance is the general patriarchal system in which men control the labor of women in virtually all aspects of American society.

A patriarchal division of labor operates in several ways. First, men rarely perform women's work. Since men's work is more important, they do not have to be involved in domestic work. Second, men attempt to control their own realm through the exclusion of women. In agricultural production, however, a contradiction emerges for male farmers. On the one hand, men attempt to exclude women from work in the agricultural realm. The hierarchical system between men farmers confers higher status to men who are able to afford to keep their wives out of agriculture. Wealthier farmers keep women out of the fields. On the other hand, many farmers are caught in a cost-price squeeze and are unable to keep women removed from agricultural production. Male farmers often need women's labor outside the home to provide cash. In many instances, women do work in the male realm of agricultural production. In these instances, men decide which work women perform.

The approach taken here can be described as follows: (1) There is an emphasis upon allowing women to speak for themselves so that one can understand the subjective experiences of women on farms. For a discussion and defense of the value of such qualitative research, see Millman and Kanter (1975). (2) The approach is historical. Understanding the daily activities of these women involves seeing their lives within the context of a social formation which has evolved over a considerable period of time. Transformations in the processes of agricultural production and changes in women's lives over time provide a background from which to comprehend the experiences of women in agriculture. (3) The book takes a feminist approach in that it offers both a description of women's subordination and a prescription for eliminating it. There is no one unique "feminist perspective," but throughout this study women's position in agriculture is examined with an eye toward the impact of political, class, and gender systems on women.

The book begins with an historical overview of changes in agricultural production in the United States focusing on how the nature of labor performed by farm women has

shifted historically. Beginning with women's work in subsistence production in seventeenth and eighteenth century
New England, Chapter 1 traces the changes in women's work
in agriculture to the present.

Women's work on farms is conditioned by the sexual
division of labor in society as well as by changes in the
agricultural production process. Chapter 2 explores how the
emphasis on women as domestic beings has kept women in
a subordinate position. The emergence of domestic ideology
is discussed, followed by an analysis of how religion, science,
capital, and the government legitimate this ideology. The
emphasis on domesticity spread from the cities to rural areas
so that there has been an increasing emphasis on domestic
work as the proper realm for farm women.

The family farm has been held up as the natural means
of agricultural production in the United States. Chapter 3
examines the changing nature of the family farm and un-
derscores the patriarchal arrangements on these farms. Patriarchal authority often pushes women into domestic rather
than farm work. Through exploring the historical roots of
patriarchal authority on the family farm, the stage is set for
examining the situation of women in agriculture.

Women *are* farmers in the United States, however overlooked they may be in studies of farming. Chapter 4 reports
the findings from a series of twenty-one in-depth interviews
with women farmers. From these interviews, the following
four types of women farmers can be identified: 1) widows,
2) single women, 3) women married to men who are not
farmers, and 4) women married to farmers. This chapter
presents two case studies for each of these types and then
discusses the constraints and possibilities facing women farmers.

Having discussed how agricultural production in the United
States is based on men's control of land, cash crops, machinery,
and of women's labor, the final chapter explores how the
male bias in the U.S. system of agriculture is transferred
throughout the world through programs of development. It
is argued that third world development has often increased
the difficulty of women's lives through excluding them from

access to modern agricultural techniques. In addition, policies which encourage the domestication of women have been transferred from the United States to many developing countries. This exclusion of women from control of agricultural production may have disastrous consequences for people throughout the world.

1

Historical Perspective

Women have participated in agricultural production in the United States since before the invasion of European settlers, but the bulk of their labor has been performed under the direct or indirect control of men. As a result, accurate information on women's work in agriculture is sketchy at best. Variations by region, crop, industrial labor demands, race, ethnicity, and class are such that there are no strict prescriptions as to what constitutes women's work on farms. With the transition from an agrarian economy in the seventeenth century to the present urban industrial economy, major changes have occurred in the agricultural production system. With these changes, the sexual division of labor in agriculture has continually shifted over time. In this book, the changing patterns of women's work on farms will be traced in the context of the overall changes in the system of agricultural production.

The historical transitions in women's work in agriculture are here examined through a review and analysis of available material. Throughout this chapter, descriptions of changes in the structure of agriculture are followed by a discussion of how these changes affect women's involvement in agriculture. The chapter begins with a discussion of women's work in subsistence production in the seventeenth and eighteenth centuries, followed by an exploration of the connection between industrialization and farm work for women. Then, regional differences in women's work are noted through a discussion of the expansion of the frontier, which provided opportunities for women that did not exist in colonial New England. The variations in women's work in agriculture in the West are examined by focusing on three groups: women married to farmers; women farmers; and women wage laborers. The situation of women on farms in the early twentieth century is described. Racial, regional, and crop variations in women's work in agriculture are discussed, focusing on cotton and tobacco production in the South. From the 1950s through the 1970s, research related to women on farms addressed the issues of sexual division of labor and decision making on farms. Review and criticism of these studies are followed by a discussion of the situation of present-day farm women.

The Beginning of an Agrarian System

From the seventeenth century to the early nineteenth century, the United States was based on an agrarian economy. The vast majority of the population lived and worked on farms or plantations where their food, clothing, and other subsistence needs were produced. The continual transformation in agricultural production in the United States has involved the expansion of commercial agriculture and a constant reduction in the proportion of the population working in agricultural production and living on farms. In 1840, 89 percent of the population was rural. Throughout the nineteenth century, there was a steady movement of people from farms to urban areas. This, combined with urban immigration, meant that by 1900 only 60 percent of the population was rural, for the most part living on farms. In 1980, 26 percent of the population was rural but less than 3 percent of the population lived on farms (U.S. Bureau of the Census, 1982). In exploring the changes in women's work in agriculture, the steadily decreasing proportion of both men and women involved in U.S. agriculture is of major significance.

SUBSISTENCE PRODUCTION IN THE
SEVENTEENTH AND EIGHTEENTH CENTURIES

The majority of people in the northern American colonies lived in isolated rural villages and were engaged in subsistence farming throughout the eighteenth century. Thus, agricultural production in the seventeeth- and eighteenth-century North was directed primarily toward providing food and goods for the family and neighbors. Although a system of local exchange existed, it was not necessarily based on the market. Exchange of local services was often based on barter with the motivation for exchange being need rather than profit (Henretta, 1978; Mutch, 1977). What commercial farming did exist in the eighteenth-century North was concentrated near the coast and near towns. The domestic urban market was supplied by farmers who lived close to the towns. In terms of agricultural production for export, U.S. international trade was quite small in the eighteenth century.

There was a division of labor both between and within families. Not every family did everything and not every family member contributed equally to each family enterprise. For example, some women made clothing, salted beef, pickled pork, or churned butter; some men were blacksmiths, carpenters, cobblers, or stonemasons (Mutch, 1977). Products and services were exchanged between families, usually without the intrusion of middlemen or a monetary transaction. Within the families, tasks were divided by sex. Men were usually responsible for field crops, large livestock, and clearing land. Women were responsible for garden crops, small livestock, and domestic production. From the seventeenth century until the present, women have worked in the field during the periods of labor shortage (Smuts, 1971; Stewart, 1961; Schob, 1975). Most sources fail to mention that the seasonal and labor-intensive character of agricultural production results in frequent periods of labor shortage. Thus, the traditional division of tasks was not rigidly adhered to. During periods of labor shortage women often peformed male tasks. The domestic tasks for which women were responsible were seldom performed by males, however. The exchange of

services between family members was not compared or measured, but simply expected. Women's economic role was
essential to the viability of the subsistence farm.

It seems clear that a sexual division of labor existed, but
there is some disagreement concerning the degree of male
dominance in colonial New England. Folbre (1980) points
out that men exerted control over their wives, sons, and
daughters on colonial New England farms. In some places,
laws required all single persons to be under the authority of
a family head. Folbre emphasizes that historically, the family
farm in the United States was characterized by patriarchal
authority. Bloch, on the other hand, notes that North American
women seeemed to be slightly more autonomous than European women. She states, "More American women—particularly heirs of deceased fathers or husbands—seem to have
owned and managed their property than was possible in the
Old World" (1978:244). Bloch also mentions that in the
colonies continual labor shortages delayed the emergence of
a rigid hierarchical differentiation of tasks. Folbre (1980)
emphasizes the patriarchal character of the subsistence farm,
while Bloch points to the advantages of women in America
compared to their European counterparts. Women in America
may have been slightly more autonomous than European
women and did often perform the same work as males, but
they continued to be under male authority.

THE TRANSITION FROM SUBSISTENCE
TO COMMERCIAL PRODUCTION

Subsistence farming, which depends on diversified production,
relies heavily on the labor of women. In early-nineteenth-
century America, there occurred a shift toward a market
orientation in both the countryside and the cities. Farm
production was increasingly geared toward cash crops. As
market-oriented farming replaced subsistence farming, men's
work in the fields was assumed to be of greater economic
importance (Ankarloo, 1979). Men's work focused on production for the market, while women produced goods and
services for home use. Although women's subsistence labor

was economically essential for the survival of the farm, women's subsistence work was undervalued because it was generally nonmarket activity. There were certain products, such as eggs and butter, that women produced and sold on the market. Women still worked in the fields, but the cash crops were generally considered to belong to the men.

In examining the transition from subsistence to commercial production, regional differences must be taken into account. American agriculture varied by region in terms of crops produced, type of labor used, landownership patterns, and market orientation. In the North, commercial production increased in conjunction with the rise of industrial production. Farmers' production was increasingly geared to providing food for urban dwellers. Compared to agriculture in the North, southern agriculture was from the outset oriented toward production for the market. The products of southern agriculture were in demand in England throughout the colonial period. The production of tobacco, rice, indigo, and sugarcane for foreign markets enabled the South to develop a commercial type of agriculture not found in the North. For example, during the colonial period, tobacco constituted one-fourth to one-half of all American exports. By 1775, 85 million pounds of tobacco were exported annually (Bogart, 1923). Commercial agricultural production in the South was accomplished on large estates with a large supply of cheap labor. In 1775, the average size of a Virginia estate was five thousand acres; in the Northeast, the average farm size was one hundred acres (Bogart, 1923).

The development of plantation agriculture was dependent upon the increased demand for cotton brought about by the industrialization processes occurring in England. As Billings states, "Plantations are parts of a wider economic system at the center of which are distant commercial and industrial cities" (1979:13). Bogart (1923) points out that the price of cotton rose from 14½ cents a pound in 1790 to 44 cents in 1799, thus stimulating increased cotton production. Due to the low level of technology, the planters needed large quantities of labor in order to increase production. Slaves had been brought to the United States from Africa as early as the seventeenth century and proved to be the solution to the problem of labor scarcity in cotton production. With the availability of land on the frontier, there was little incentive for free people to enter employment (Thompson, 1975). A system of forced labor was therefore "developed in response to the effects of the frontier on the southern labor supply" ('Billings, 1979:17). Europeans preferred Africans as slaves over American Indians; indigenous slave labor is always in short supply due to difficulties of control (Wallerstein, 1974). In addition, the hunting and gathering economy of the Indians meant that the population was low and not available for wage labor. Because the South was a plantation society throughout most of the nineteenth century, the dependence on external markets for agricultural products occurred earlier in the South than in the North or West. The South was dominated by the plantation system, but the fact that many small farmers existed should not be overlooked. As Genovese suggests, "The concentration of land and slaveholding prevented the rise of a prosperous yeomanry and/or urban centers" (1961:34). The situation of the yeoman farmers in the South was quite unlike that of their northern counterparts. The small southern farmers were dominated and tied to the plantations. According to Genovese, "The plantation offered virtually the only market for the small nonstaple-producing farmers and provided the center of necessary services for the small cotton growers. Thus, the paternalism of the planters toward their slaves was reinforced by the semipaternal relationship between the planters and their neighbors" (1961:30–31).

The southern plantation economy relied on the heavy labor of black women and men to produce agricultural commodities. Eighty percent of slave women worked in the fields; the remaining 20 percent were primarily house servants (Fogel and Engerman, 1974). Girls went to the fields with their parents at the age of twelve, and in several years were involved in planting, plowing, hoeing, and harvesting (Jensen, 1981). Genovese points out that during slavery, women field hands worked longer days than the men. "In addition to the usual work load, the women had to cook for their families, put the children to bed, and often spin, weave, and sew well into the night. On many plantations masters and overseers released them from fieldwork early to attend to their household chores, but on many others they did not, except perhaps on Saturday to get the week's washing done" (1974:495).

Although both men and women worked in the fields together, a sexual division of labor existed. The women were responsible for the domestic tasks, whereas the men usually did the plowing. In addition to their agricultural production for the plantation and their families, women slaves were also valued as breeders of slaves. The value of a woman slave was measured both by her field production capacity and childbearing capacity (Brown, 1976; Fogel and Engerman, 1974). Slave women were often pregnant while working. Usually, the masters lightened the woman's work load for a month before childbirth and expected her to resume her full work load a month after delivery (Genovese, 1972).

From Farm to Factory

Women's work on the farm was interconnected with emerging industrialization. In order to comprehend the lives of rural women in the early nineteenth century, it is important to explore the connections between farm work and factory work. Industrialization in New England first occurred in the realm of textile production. Prior to industrialization, cloth production was primarily the work of women in the home.

Women and children were the initial providers of labor for the establishment of American industrialism. While many women eventually went into the factories, there was resistance to the routinized work in factories. Nash describes how an attempt to establish a spinning factory in Boston in 1750 ended in failure. The goal, which was to hire women and children to perform spinning and weaving in a factory, was not reached, primarily due to women's reluctance to work for low wages in a factory. As Nash explains, "They would spin at home, working as time allowed to produce what they could within the rhythm of their daily routine and accepting small piecework wages. But removal to an institutional setting, even for daytime labor, involved a new kind of labor discipline and separation of productive and reproductive responsibilities that challenged deeply rooted values" (1979:180–181).

The first plant in America for carding and spinning yarn was established in 1789 in Rhode Island. By 1800 an organized cotton industry existed, with fifteen mills in Massachusetts, Rhode Island, and Connecticut. Until 1814, only yarn was manufactured in the mills; yarn was then sent out to women in their homes to be woven on hand looms (Baker, 1964). Henretta (1978) describes the period from 1775 to 1815 as the heyday of domestic manufacture.

In a 1791 report on manufactures, Secretary of the Treasury Alexander Hamilton "hailed factory employment for women because it made development of the new system possible without taking men from the fields" (Baker, 1964:5). Women continued to perform the work of textile production through following production from the home to the mill. For example, in 1827 nine-tenths of the twelve hundred persons employed at the Lowell, Massachusetts mills were girls and women (Baker, 1964).

With an increasing need for cash income for families by the early 1800s, women were working in factories. The majority of the workers in these factories were young farm women who moved to mill towns to work. "They were working outside the home, but not for themselves as un-attached individuals" (Henretta, 1978:32). Alexander Hamilton noticed that the work of mill girls could provide income for men farmers. As he stated, "The husband-man himself experiences a new source of profit and support, from the increased industry of his wives and daughters" (Baker, 1964:6).

Dublin (1975) has described the work and living situation of the women in the mills at Lowell. The women worked together and lived together in company-owned boarding houses. While the initiation to mill work was a difficult transition for the young rural women, they frequently found a support group of other women to assist them in their first weeks in the mills. In Lowell, women had more social and intellectual opportunities than they had experienced in rural areas. Women who worked in the mills experienced feelings of ambiguity toward both the mills and the country. A woman's letter to her friend at Lowell reflects an understanding of the contradictions of life in the town and the country:

> I suppose you have by this time become naturalized to Lowell and become accustomed to the din and clatter of machinery. . . . Doubtless you sometimes cast a wistful glance to your country home when the bright sun is shining cheerily forth and nature is alive with beauties, but in a few weeks you will be thankful that you are not buried up in impenetrable snowbanks and obliged to make your own paths through drifts of snow. Give me the country in the summer, but I would prefer when winter comes to be situated in some place where all the avenues to enjoyment do not seem to be frozen up. [as quoted in Wolfe, 1976:98]

Women's experience in the mills involved elaborate shifts in their lives. The movement from farm to town was in itself dramatic. Work in the mills was based on timed labor rather than completion of tasks (see Thompson, 1967). Young women were physically removed from their families and their fathers' authority. Rather than living with family members they lived with young women. They continued to work under male authority, but the males were now employers rather than family members.

Dublin explains the contradictory impact of women's employment in the mills on the lives of these women:

> The experiences of Lowell women before 1850 present a fascinating picture of the contradictory impact of industrial capitalism. Repeated labor protests reveal that female operatives felt the demands of mill employment to be oppressive. At the same time, however, the mills provided women with work outside of the home and family, thereby offering them an unprecedented [opportunity]. That they came to challenge employer paternalism was a direct consequence of the increasing opportunities offered them in these years. The Lowell mills both exploited and liberated women in ways unknown to the pre-industrial economy. [1975:116]

The types of labor that women performed in the mills and

on the farm are intimately related. In contrast to England and the Continent, where women worked as reapers and mowers, it was not customary for women to work in the fields in New England (E. Abbott, 1910). Young women were certainly engaged in productive labor, but the goods they produced were generally for home consumption. With the growth of industrial capitalism and a switch to market-oriented farming, farm families needed cash to survive. The work that young, unmarried women performed on the farm became less and less valuable on the market as domestic production shifted from the home to the factory.

Fathers looked to their sons to provide agricultural labor. The proponents of industrialization attempted to convince these men that their daughters could also be valuable to them. An address to the Convention of the Friends of Domestic Industry in 1831 extols the benefits of farmers' daughters working for wages: "Daughters are now emphatically a blessing to the farmer. Many instances have occurred within the personal knowledge of individuals of this committee in which the earning of daughters have been scrupulously hoarded to enable them to pay off mortgages on the parental farm" (as quoted in E. Abbott, 1910:55). Young women who worked in the mills did not have control over their earnings. While they experienced physical separation from the patriarchal authority in their families, their labor remained the property of their fathers.

Daughters of farm families had traditionally assisted their mothers on the farm. Cott explains that the daughters worked with the housewives in "food preparation and preservation, dairying, gardening, cleaning, laundering, soapmaking, candle making, knitting, and textile and clothing manufacture" (1977:26). The work load of the mothers on the farm increased as their daughters assumed employment in the mills. While there was tremendous interdependency in the farm household, the man on the farm was more likely to benefit from his daughter's work than was her mother, who lost her helper.

Once women married, they usually returned to farms. Into the middle decades of the nineteenth century, married women's work centered around the household and family care.

As Cott points out, however, the growing importance "of the market economy diminished the importance of household manufacture and enlarged families' reliance on money to purchase basic commodities" (1977:43). With the development of a market economy, women's limited access to economic power served to widen the economic gap between men and women. Women continued to perform labor that was not readily exchangeable on the market—household duties, child-rearing tasks, and production and preservation of the family food supply. Jensen (1980) notes that male farmers abandoned the philosophy of self-sufficiency long before farm women did. The farm itself was defined more in terms of the man's work. Women raised food and brought in cash from egg and butter sales, but increasingly the major emphasis on the farm was the male's cash crops.

Landownership and Women

Land is a major factor in agricultural production. Patterns of landownership in the United States have been instrumental in shaping the type of agricultural production and women's role in agriculture. Historically, small-scale farms owned, managed, and worked by a family were predominant in U.S. agriculture (Goss, Rodefeld, and Buttel, 1980). Compared to the solidified pattern of landownership in feudal Europe, land in America was more evenly divided. However, the picture of America as a land occupied by yeoman farmers, each owning a sufficient amount of land, has often been overdrawn. Rather, from the outset of European occupation of America, land has been unequally divided. As Ryan (1979) notes, agrarian society in America was not without poverty, tenancy, or a landed aristocracy.

Patterns of landownership varied by region and over time. Paul Gates (1979) argues that the pattern of landownership in America was established through the early colonial land grants of the French, British, and Spanish. Variation of landownership patterns ranged from narrow strip farming to large plantations to huge speculative tracts.

While agriculture in the northern United States in the

eighteenth century was performed largely on small subsistence farms, an inequitable land ownership pattern existed. For example, a study focusing on landholding and tenancy patterns in six New Jersey towns in the late eighteenth century found marginality and tenancy to be pervasive (Ryan, 1979). According to Ryan's calculations, approximately one-third of all adult males had marginal holdings of less than fifty acres, another one-third were landless, and only 35 percent of taxpayers in six towns in 1778 possessed enough land to meet the subsistence needs of their families. The marginal landholders and the landless either rented land or members of the farm household worked in the fields of more prosperous neighbors. This pattern of land tenancy and marginality was typical of many areas in the northeast (Gates, 1960).

While land was unevenly distributed among men, women had relatively minimal access to land. Although families worked together on farms, men owned the land. Fathers controlled the land, determining its use and how it was to be distributed to their sons. The majority of sons did not achieve economic independence until after their fathers' deaths (Folbre, 1980), when land was transferred to them. Women rarely achieved economic independence at all. Daughters could not expect to inherit land except in the absence of sons. If a woman did inherit land, it became the property of her husband when she married. Prior to the nineteenth century, widows had no control over their families' land. During the nineteenth century, women gained the right to own land after their husband's death and to dispose of it as they would (Jensen, 1981).

The Movement West

During the early nineteenth century, more land became available for settlement by United States citizens. The continuous availability of new land in the United States through the annexation of French and Spanish territories and the usurpation of Indian lands, combined with the pressure of the market and the lack of available land in the East, led many families to establish farms in the West. The movement west was usually initiated by men (Schlissel, 1978), but the struggle involved in the trip frequently resulted in the breaking down of the traditional sexual division of labor. According to Faragher and Stansell (1975), women experienced the breakdown of the sexual division of labor as the dissolution of their own sphere. Women performed men's work, but men seldom reciprocated. Although women's traditional domestic work was performed for the benefit of men and children, women experienced some degree of independence from patriarchal authority in this "women's sphere." The opportunity to move out of the domestic sphere was not always viewed as liberating for women. As Faragher and Stansell note, "The Trail, in breaking down sexual segregation, offered women the opportunities of socially essential work. Yet this work was performed in a male arena, and many women saw themselves as draftees rather than partners" (1975:161).

On the frontier, women were expected to work with their husbands until the homestead was established. During the first years on the land, women planted, harvested, and built. "Later, as more settlers moved in, as the farm prospered in good years, and as . . . sons grew older, the heavy field work was taken over by men" (Smuts, 1971:7). Women in general were workers rather than partners.

Women have always worked in the fields during periods of labor shortage, but rarely has their domestic workload decreased in relation to their involvement in field work. The answer to the question, Why have women been excluded from field work in American agriculture? lies beyond the explanation of patriarchal control or women's child-rearing duties. Married women were expected to perform certain domestic, farm, and child-rearing tasks regardless of the extent of their involvement in field work. One avenue of resistance open to women was to refuse to work in the field. They were able to claim their own realm where they did not work directly under their husbands. Jeffrey (1979), approaching her study of women on the frontier with the presupposition that the impact of the frontier on these women enabled them to break down traditional sexual divisions of labor, found that they attempted to reestablish the forms of the domestic world that characterized their lives in the East.

These studies of women on the frontier emphasize women's attempt to reestablish their own sphere. In addition, males have benefited from and encouraged the sexual division of labor on the farm. Patriarchal authority relies to some extent on the exclusion of women from the male realm. Both patriarchal control and women's resistance to this control perpetuated the reestablishment of the sexual division of labor on the frontier.

LAND IN THE WEST

Henretta (1978) notes that the renewed expropriation of Indian land in the early nineteenth century brought about a partial reversal of the pattern of increased tenancy that had begun to develop. Within a few decades, however, a pattern of land wealth in the frontier states developed that was similar to that in the East. The farmer of limited means faced many difficulties in achieving landownership even on the frontier. Prior to and immediately following the annexation of various territories, land speculators laid claim to land and made large purchases. While the policies of the federal government in the first half of the nineteenth century were explicitly designed to encourage the settlement of land by small farmers, land speculation was rampant, and undermined the Jeffersonian ideal of an agrarian democracy. The policies of the federal government were often overridden through corruption and dominance of the large landholders in various states and localities (Richardson, 1979). Many settlers moved to neighboring states with the belief that public land was readily available. For example, an article in the *Missouri Gazette* in 1816 exclaimed, "Come one, Come all, we have millions of acres to occupy, and provisions are cheap and in abundance." (as quoted in Richardson, 1979). People who migrated in response to these claims found that the only land for sale was in the hands of speculators. Often families were unable to afford land, or speculators were unwilling to sell, the result being a preponderance of tenant farmers.

The government's ideal of disposing of public land for use rather than sale was continued in the Homestead Act of 1862. The major difference in this act compared to previous policy was that land was free rather than for sale as a source of government revenue. Any farmer who was willing to live on the land and develop it was entitled to a piece of land not in excess of 160 acres. On the surface the Homestead Act appeared to support the ideal of a sufficient plot of land for every willing family, but much of the good public land was already disposed of prior to the passage of the Act. As Shannon explains, "Most of the choice land in the country (land suited for general agriculture, and having sufficient rainfall to assure crops) had been picked over before the Homestead Act was passed" (1936:638).

Many historians suggest that by 1890 the frontier was settled and the best lands had been claimed largely through the dispersion of land made possible by the Homestead Act. However, Shannon (1936) questions the success of the Homestead Act, examining the relative size of the territory distributed and noting the tendency of the best land to fall into the hands of larger landowners. In the first place, by 1890 only 372,659 homesteads had actually been titled. The total land these homesteads encompassed was approximately 3½ percent of the total territory west of the Mississippi River. While the government maintained its policy of providing free land for the actual settler, state policy was contradictory: by 1890, four times the amount of land given to private individuals had been granted to railroad companies (Shannon, 1936). Although small parcels of free land were made legally available with the passage of the Homestead Act, much of the private land was already concentrated. An additional problem with the Homestead Act was that Congress did nothing to insure its implementation. As Shannon explains, "Congress merely adopted the law and then did nothing in the way of helping needy persons out to the land or extending them credit and guidance in the first heartbreaking years of occupancy . . . [without this the] Homestead Act could benefit only monopolists or persons of fairly ample means" (1936:644).

In fact, the Public Land Commission made the following

statements approximately thirty years after the passage of the Homestead Act: "In very many localities, and perhaps in general, a larger proportion of the public land is passing into the hands of speculators and corporations than into those of actual settlers who are making their homes." And further, "Nearly everywhere the large landowner has succeeded in monopolizing the best tracts, whether of timber or agricultural land" (Shannon, 1936:646). According to Cramer (1972:646), Land Office officials reported the following amounts of land given or sold to speculators and corporations by 1900:

To Railroads	181,000,000 acres
To States	140,000,000 acres
Direct Sales by the Land Office	100,000,000 acres
Sale of Indian Lands	100,000,000 acres
TOTAL	521,000,000 acres

Cramer notes that half a billion acres passed into the hands of monopolists while homesteaders had actually received only 80 million acres. With this type of land distribution, tenancy soon began to replace yeoman farming.

WOMEN ON WESTERN FARMS

Despite tenancy patterns that favored large landholders, women in the West had more opportunity to own land and participate in agriculture. In addition to the married women who resisted male authority through creation of a women's sphere, a number of women farmed on their own in the West. Smuts (1971) notes that in the last quarter of the nineteenth century, a quarter of a million women ran farms of their own. The majority of these women were widows; others had husbands who were no longer able to work; and some were single women who owned land.

Documentation of women farmers is rare; scattered information indicates their presence. For example, these exerpts from Penny's book on women's work in the 1860s notes the existence of women farmers. "We have heard of women in

Western New York, Ohio, and Michigan, that not only carry on farms but do the outdoor work, as tilling, reaping, etc. . . . There are two sisters in Ohio who manage a farm of 300 acres; and two other sisters, near Media, Pennsylvania, that conduct as large a farm . . . Mrs. D. owns a farm, and does not disdain to graft fruit trees, superintend their planting, gather fruit, send it to market, etc.; and she realizes a handsome profit" (1863:136,137,142).

In addition to women who worked on farms owned by themselves or their husbands, a number of young women worked on farms as hired labor. "Hired girls" were usually domestic assistants to the women on farms. Often, these hired girls were newly arrived immigrants. Schob explains that "normally women did not engage in field tasks" (1975:196). But shortage of labor was common, such that few harvesting seasons were "normal," and a number of these hired girls did perform field work.

The letters of Elinor Pruitt Stewart describe the life and work of a woman homesteader and hired worker. Stewart had been a domestic worker in Denver. She left Denver with her young daughter to work and buy land in the mountains of Utah. In Utah, she filed a claim on land and built a house adjoining that of her employer, whom she later married. She described the labor shortage on the frontier:

> Help of any kind is very hard to get here, and Mr. Stewart had been too confident of getting men, so that haying caught him with too few men to put up the hay. He had no man to run the mower and he couldn't run both the mower and stacker, so you can fancy what a place he was in.[1961:16]

Stewart explained that due to the early death of her parents she had learned to operate the mowing machine in order to keep her family together. As a young girl, she had found this work unappealing because she had been told that performing such work would diminish her opportunities for marrying a man. She wrote of her mowing work:

> It cost me many bitter tears because I got sunburned, and my hands were hard, rough and stained with machine oil, and I used to wonder how any Prince Charming could overlook all

that in any girl he came to. For all I had ever read of the Prince had to do with his "reverently kissing her lily-white hand," or doing some other fool trick with a hand as white as a snowflake. [1961:16]

During the labor shortage, she recalled her ability to mow but felt it would be inappropriate for her to suggest this to her employer:

I was afraid to tell him I could mow for fear he would forbid me to do so. But one morning, when he was chasing a last hope of help, I went down to the barn, took out the horses, and went to mowing. I had enough cut before he got back to show him I knew how, and as he came back manless he was delighted as well as surprised. I was glad because I really like to mow, and besides that, I am adding feathers to my cap in a surprising way. When you see me again you will think I am wearing a feather duster, it is only that I have been said to have almost as much sense as a "mon" (man), and that is an honor I never aspired to, even in my wildest dreams. [1961:17]

In describing her participation in field work, Elinor Stewart reveals the contradictory feelings of both women and men toward women's work in the fields. On the one hand, women were discouraged from doing "men's work" because it made them less feminine, that is, unattractive to men. Also, they had to continue to perform "women's work" regardless of their participation in "men's work." On the other hand, many women enjoyed working outdoors. Men were in need of workers, but preferred male workers to women workers. As the letters convey, men had the authority to "forbid" women to work in the fields. Despite the wishes of women, men usually had control over the labor process. But as Elinor Stewart's entry into the fields indicates, women resisted this control. Women, because of men's authority, remain aware of men's definition of their proper role. The adolescent fear of being unattractive to men because of her work in the fields was transformed in Stewart's adult years to men defining her as having almost as much sense as a man.

Schob describes the work of a Norwegian woman immigrant who worked for a Norwegian farmer in Wisconsin, as a

" 'Handy-Andy' for the men in the fields, including manual labor during harvest, when she rode the back of the reaper raking hay on the platform like any common harvest hand. Rainy days she devoted to domestic chores like baking and churning" (1975:198–199).

As large-scale specialized farming replaced the frontier subsistence economy, the demand for labor was initially more pronounced. The move toward specialized wheat production required vast numbers of hired workers during harvest. Labor was often supplied by newly arrived immigrants, both male and female. The mechanical reaper quickly replaced immigrant labor in the wheat fields, however. Schob (1975) notes that the mechanical reaper was not widely accepted prior to 1850, but by 1860, 50 percent of the wheat in Illinois was harvested by machines.

The shortage of labor in the Midwest included a shortage of women. Specialization began on Midwest farms in the 1840s and 1850s. Dairy farms in Wisconsin and Illinois needed the labor of young women. An article in the *Illinois Farmer* in 1857 stated, "What we want is a supply of young women from the butter regions of Eastern States to come here and also from the Dairy Districts of England, Scotland, Ireland, and Germany" (as quoted in Schob, 1975:199). Milking cows was women's work.

Although most field work was considered "men's work," black, immigrant, or poor women often performed field labor. An 1871 report of the commissioner of agriculture of the United States describes the work of immigrant women in various sections of the country. At the same time, this report emphasizes that white American women on well-to-do farms seldom engage in field work.

> Very little farm work is done by native Americans [whites] in all the States of the Ohio Valley and the Lakes, that little being casual assistance in emergencies, as a matter of convenience and sometimes of necessity. . . . Immigrants do more outdoor work, especially for a few years after coming here. As they become Americanized they work less on the farm.
>
> Canadian women, and occasionally Irish, hire out or work on

shares in different parts of New England, though the number employed is not large, and they will undertake nearly all kinds of farm work. "Many of them are as smart as men," but as a rule they are less efficient and receive proportionately less pay.

In many districts in Pennsylvania very little outdoor employment is undertaken by women, while in others, especially in those less improved, or with a large foreign element in the population, much and various farm work is done by women.

In Minnesota female immigrants work extensively in all branches of farming. "In hulling and shucking of grain, some of them are equal to the best of men." [Holmes, 1912a:27–29]

While field work was generally considered inappropriate for white American women, work in particular crops such as hops, grapes, and berries was considered appropriate for them. The commissioner of agriculture's report for 1871 explained that girls were exclusively employed in picking hops because of their nimble fingers (Holmes, 1912a:27). In hiring workers for grape cultivation, farm owners also utilized women. German immigrants were often hired to cultivate grapes because their wives and daughters performed much of the work (Schob, 1975).

Thus, despite the oft-stated claim that women seldom performed field work, scattered evidence indicates that women often did work in the fields. Although reports from the late nineteenth century suggest that field work was considered "men's work," there seem to have been many instances in which women performed it. It was appropriate for women to work in the fields for hire during periods of labor shortage, in particular crops, or if they were black, immigrants, or poor. The defining of field work as "inappropriate" for white women, in addition to the tendency of farmers and authors to devalue women's labor, may well have resulted in the underreporting of women's contribution to agricultural production.

Urbanization, Industrialization, and Women on Farms

With increased industrialization and the gradual transformation of products previously produced in the household into commodities, the situation of rural women altered. Until the end of the nineteenth century, women produced and processed food and other goods that were consumed on the farm. Household production also afforded women the opportunity to sell their goods on the market. For example, many farm women relied on the sale of their butter as a source of cash income. Braverman (1974) notes that in 1879 almost all butter was produced on farms, in 1899 the proportion was under three-fourths, and by 1939 only one-fifth of butter was made on farms. Because of the continual commodification of their products, women became less able to contribute cash to the farm enterprise at a time when the need for cash on the farm had increased. As Braverman explains, "During the last hundred years industrial capital has thrust itself between farm and household, and appropriated all the processing functions of both, thus extending the commodity form to food in its semiprepared or even fully prepared forms" (1974:274).

Industrial capital was aided in this process through the passage of laws that regulated or forbade home production in garment, tobacco, and food industries (Smuts, 1971). These laws were passed to protect against sweatshops, but they also encouraged the concentration of products. In addition, the cheapening of manufactured goods, made possible through the extraction of surplus value from workers in factories, made home production inefficient. Women's production in the home was continually removed to the factories through economic and legal means.

A USDA report published in 1912 attests to the decline in home production.

> The old-time domestic industries are all but forgotten. The women of the farm make no more soap, candles, or lye, and so on with a long list of the domestic products of former days; it is rare that one of the younger of the women knows how to knit. Throughout large areas the pride of the housewife in great store of preserved, dried, and pickled fruits, berries, and vegetables exists chiefly as history, and dependence is placed mostly upon the local store for the products of the cannery and the evaporator. [Holmes, 1912b:70]

The extension of the commodity form increased the need for cash on the farm in order to purchase farm inputs, machinery, and household goods. Women and girls were less able than ever to earn cash through their production activities on the farm. Therefore, between 1870 and 1900, many girls on farms in the Midwest were sent away at an early age (Ankarloo, 1979). Boys remained on farms to work in agricultural production.

Young women led the migration from the farm to the city in the early twentieth century. Family farms were unable to keep all of their members on the farm. As Ankarloo explains, "In families forced to send away children at an early age, girls were the first to go" (1979:118). Since farm families were based on patriarchal authority, the male farmers usually opted for retaining sons rather than encouraging daughters to remain to work with the farm women. Women's labor was frequently devalued because much of it was production for use rather than for exchange. As girls were sent away, the work load of the farm woman increased. Women no longer had their daughters to help them with their work.

At the same time that families sent young girls off the farm, the disadvantages of farm life for women were becoming apparent to women who lived on farms. Farm women's lives were characterized by isolation and hard work. Male farmers utilized the cash from their agricultural sales to reinvest in machines and labor-saving devices for outdoor work rather than for household items. Kitchen and household items were considered luxuries. Chandler described the situation on farms in 1918: "Barns may contain every device for effective, easy work, while houses are as primitive as those of the pioneers" (1918:34). He explained that the farm man felt justified in purchasing equipment that helped him because he could expect a direct cash return on his investment. A report of the U.S. Country Life Commission summed up the situation of women on farms: "Whatever general hardships, such as poverty, isolation, lack of labor-saving devices, may exist on any given farm, the burden of these hardships falls more heavily on the farmer's wife than on the farmer himself" (1911:104).

Governmental concern with the situation of rural women was based on a need to have a class permanently attached to the land (Chandler, 1918) and on demands raised by women in conjunction with the strengthening women's movement in the early twentieth century. As women realized that their oppressive work conditions were due to the exercise of male authority, they were less content to remain on the farm and perform never-ending labor. Life in the towns and cities seemed more appealing to many.

In the first decades of the twentieth century, the government, particularly the Department of Agriculture, attempted to counter claims that farm life was disadvantageous to women. For example, a bulletin published by the USDA in 1912 attempted to prove that farm women were not plagued by insanity. The report stated that "for many years the published statement has been current that farm life has made the women of the farm especially prone to insanity" (Holmes, 1912b:71). The author cited the testimony of an asylum superintendent to disprove this assertion. During the next decade, the USDA supported a study called "The Advantages of Farm Life," which was based on correspondence and interviews with eight thousand farm women. The author of this report initiated the study in an attempt to reveal the fallacy of the popular conception of farm life for women as drudgery.

The USDA realized that women were a major influence in maintaining a class that was attached to the land. A 1918 article explained that importance of farm women: "In the long run, she is more important than fertilizers or feed, farm labor or seeds, and her importance does not lie chiefly in the work of her hands, though this is of vital necessity, but in her love or hatred of the farm, her appraisal of the worthwhileness or utter distastefulness of rural life" (Chandler, 1918:30). Chandler explained that the USDA had always attempted to make the farmer a prosperous man and now had to turn to the job of helping the farmer's wife and daughter to be content.

The dissatisfaction of women with rural life resulted from overwork, isolation, devaluation of work, poverty, and male dominance. In order to combat this dissatisfaction, the government, through the USDA and the schools, attempted to convince women and girls of the importance of domestic work. If women were overworked, they could resolve their problem through the rationalization of housework. The problem was defined as a lack of organization on the part of women, rather than a result of a daily routine focused on providing for the needs of husbands and children.

Women in the South

Women have historically been more active in agricultural work in the South than in other regions of the country. In the early twentieth century cotton and tobacco were important southern labor-intensive cash crops. The labor of women in cotton and tobacco is described in two excellent studies conducted in the 1930s, one by Ruth Allen (1931) and the other by Margaret Hagood (1977). Black women's labor in agriculture is markedly different than the labor of white women, and in order to comprehend women's work in agriculture, this racial distinction must be explored.

With the legal end of the slavery system, southern planters were forced to design new modes of labor control. The major mode of production after the Civil War was the sharecropping system. Blacks sharecropped or rented land from the white planters who had previously been their owners. The lives of black sharecroppers were similar to the lives of slaves. Black families barely earned subsistence and continued to work for and be dependent on white plantation owners.

Black women continued to labor in the fields on farms where sharecropping was the primary mode of production, but as Jensen points out, "they spent more time occupied in duties similar to those of Euro-American farm women" (1981:73). While child rearing and household chores had previously been shared or performed by older black women, the women were now more likely to be in nuclear family households where each woman was responsible for her own household. Jensen (1981) explains that sharecropping seemed a better alternative to black women than working for wages in the fields or the towns.

The notion in the United States that agricultural production is men's work is undermined when the labor of black women is considered. Black women in this country have always worked in the fields, and there was no attempt to keep black women out of the fields. When women's labor is needed in agricultural production, it is utilized. White men preferred to have white women in the home rather than in the fields. The racial distinction between women's work reveals that the desire to keep white women out of the fields is not based on the presumption that women cannot perform agricultural labor; rather, it is a matter of status for white men that they can keep their women in the home.

WOMEN IN THE COTTON FIELDS

Black women worked in the cotton fields as slaves and later as sharecroppers. Sara Brooks describes her work as a girl in the early 1900s. "We'd take our hoe on our sholder, and we'd have on our straw hats, and we'd be choppin corn or choppin cotton. That's what we'd be doin in the summer. Or we'd be hoein peanuts—we had to keep the grass cleaned out. And, oh, the row'd be so long! To be in the field hoein, it was awful to look from one end of the row to the other after the sun gets hot. . . . I'd hate that cotton start to open; pickin cotton was the tiredest thing" (Brooks and Simonsen, 1980:54, 58).

In *The Labor of Women in the Production of Cotton*, Allen (1931) described the work of white, black, and Mexican women working in the Texas cotton fields in the 1920s. Her discussion of white women's work is insightful, despite the fact that her description of black women's work is a racist interpretation. Of the women in her study, 46 percent of the white women were field workers, compared to 57 percent of the Mexican women and 87 percent of the black women. Thus, black women were more likely to work in the fields than Mexican women or white women.

The work of women in the fields consisted primarily of

chopping cotton, hoeing corn, and picking cotton. Of the 664 white women in Allen's study, 46.2 percent performed field work. In her discussion of white women's field work, Allen (1931) distinguished among women who worked as hired laborers, as both hired and family labor, and as family labor only. Women not tied to the land through ownership or tenancy of their families were debarred from adding cash to the family income through household production, and therefore had to work in the fields. Women who lived on farms operated by their families added cash to the family income through egg and butter production. Women who worked for wages and also for their families worked the longest hours. These women were often young unmarried women who worked to contribute cash to the family income. They were also expected to work as needed on their families' farms. In cases of economic need, married women also performed field work for wages on other farms.

Women who performed field work for their own families essentially worked as unpaid laborers. As Allen noted, "It is practically a universal situation that the money received for the sale of the crop is the man's income" (1931:147). Although he might spend it on the family, he controlled the money. Women did not receive wages for their field work, nor were they relieved of housekeeping responsibilities. While women might have preferred outdoor work to household work, the performance of field work added an additional burden onto their heavy work load.

The work of women on farms included the care of large numbers of children. Owners hiring tenant families preferred large families who could supply more labor. The importance of children as a supply of labor is linked to women's subordinate position on the farm: "In a large part of the agricultural economy of the South the importance of children as a force of workers, while making a woman an indispensable adjunct to a farm, tends also to place her in a subordinate position as a means to an end and, in the case of many farmers, degrades the mother to the position of a breeder of a labor supply" (Allen, 1931:71).

In her attempt to explore the type of work that women

performed in the fields, Allen (1931) found an ideological adherence to a strict division between women's and men's work. She explained that it was difficult to get information from women about their contribution to plowing, harrowing, or cultivating because they were often ashamed about performing these tasks. The distinction between women's and men's work in cotton is not, however, based on men doing the heavy labor: "On one side lies hoeing corn and chopping and picking cotton for the women; on the other lies riding a plow or cultivator for the men" (Allen, 1931:142). There is little question that riding a plow or a cultivator is the easiest work in the field. Therefore, "The real reason for the distinction is probably economic, and the idea of chivalric protection of women from unsuitable work, combined with the prestige aura, was developed later" (Allen, 1931:142–143).

In conclusion, Allen (1931) suggested that women should refuse to perform field work for no wages. An increase in hired labor would remedy the situation of farm women. Women cannot be expected to remain on the farm when they are physically, spiritually, and emotionally drained. In terms of farm policy, Allen (1931) accentuated the importance of recognizing the contribution of all family members to the farm enterprise.

WOMEN IN TOBACCO

Hagood's (1977) insightful study of white tenant farm women in the South in the 1930s provides a rich description of their lives. She interviewed 129 women in the Piedmont area of North Carolina and 125 women from the Deep South. Tobacco was the cash crop on three-fourths of the farms, cotton on one-fifth, and truck and miscellaneous crops on the remaining farms. Hagood was not primarily interested in the agricultural aspects of the women's lives and was surprised at their knowledge of and involvement in farming. She described women's interest in the farm:

> While the women yield to their husbands the prerogative of planning and managing the farm, of assigning tasks and directing

the family's labor on it, of selling the crop at their own discretion and pocketing the proceeds, they nevertheless have an active interest in the farms and crops often exceeding that in the home. Their knowledge of farming matters is surprising and pertains not only to the immediate condition of the current crop but to details of renting, credit, and sequence of operations, and to the basic data for making an estimate of how they will "come out this year." [1977:77]

Farm women performed a considerable amount of field work. Hagood explained that women

do as nearly full-time work as housekeeping and cooking permit during chopping, hoeing, and picking times on the cotton farm, or during most of the summer on the tobacco farm, with the fall spent largely in the striphouse. [1977:86]

She noted that the amount of work that a woman performed varied with the number, age, and sex of her children. (Women took half a day or one day a week from field work to perform their families' washing.)

Seven-eighths of the women preferred field work to household work, although many described the difficulty of performing field work, child rearing, *and* household work. Preference for field work over housework often was explained by the desire for companionship. Field work also was preferable because it could be finished, whereas housework was never-ending. The women who identified with "town women" insisted that they had no knowledge of the farming operation and believed women should spend all their time in homemaking. In one of these cases, the woman later complimented her daughter for doing all the cooking the week before, while she had worked on getting the tobacco in the barn (1977:79). A contradiction exists between housework and field work for women both in terms of time and ideology.

In another study of women on tobacco farms, Janiewski describes the family system involved in tobacco production. Women performed a large amount of labor, but men maintained control. "Whether a woman worked only in the household, worked only in tobacco but not in other crops, labored in the fields all year, or did 'public work,' her labor symbolized the ability of her household's male head to provide for the family and protect the women" (1980:19). As Janiewski describes the family system of survival, "Under the leadership of the male head, the family economy blended patriarchal forms with the emerging market economy" (1980:17).

Allen (1931) mentioned the importance of farm women as reproducers of the labor force. Compared to Allen's interest in agricultural labor, Hagood (1977) was primarily interested in women's role as mothers. The large number of children that the women in Hagood's study bore meant that much of their time was spent in child rearing. The mean number of children of the married women in her sample was 6.4. She found that the women were proud of the children they had borne, but most hoped not to have any more. The pride came from the extension of the self in producing a large family, evidence of fertility and the man's virility, and the provision of field workers of economic value for the family and society. While proud of their children, the women were also aware of the large amount of physical work in raising children, as well as the physiological and economic difficulties involved.

Decision Making and the Sexual Division of Labor on Family Farms

In the early twentieth century, when farm women had large numbers of children, much of their work involved child-rearing activities. As farms became less labor-intensive, the economic value of children to the farm operation decreased. The demands of household production changed with fewer numbers of children, but white women's primary realm of activity continued to be in domestic work. Although the demands of household production decreased, women were expected to spend more time in cleaning and child care.

In 1937, Beers (1937) reported that the family farm was moving away from the patriarchal authority that had existed on pioneer farms. According to his study, women were consulted in some decisions, especially decisions related to borrowing money. However, decisions such as whether to purchase equipment or what crops to plant were usually made by the husband. He suggested that as farms become more commercialized, decision making and the division of labor would become more specialized, with men involved in farm decisions and women involved in the home. As Beers stated, "The tendency for husbands to be solely responsible for financial decisions is more marked in families on large than on small farm enterprises. There is a suggestion in the evidence that as standards of competitive business efficiency enter farming, the splitting of executive responsibility into home and farm divisions may become more pronounced" (1937:592). While Beers claimed that the family farm had become less patriarchal, he also noted that male control of the farming operations was increasing, especially on large, commercial farms.

From the 1950s through the early 1970s, a number of studies addressed the issues of decision making and the division of labor in farm families. These studies seemed to have evolved from two distinct sources. One group of studies occurred as the agricultural extension services were emphasizing an approach known as "farm and home development" or the "farm and home unit approach" (Wilkening, 1958). Extension programs were emphasizing the importance of both the husband and wife on the family farm. Therefore a number of studies attempted to understand how the decision-making process and the sexual division of labor on the farm actually operated (Sawer, 1973; Straus, 1958, 1960; Wilkening, 1958; Wilkening and Bharadwaj, 1967, 1968; Wilkening and Morrison, 1963). At approximately the same time, other studies compared the sexual division of labor and decision making between urban and rural families (Blood, 1958; Burchinal and Bauder, 1965).

In terms of decision making, a major finding was that the husband assumed the major role in decisions concerning farm business, but there appeared to be joint decision making when other major farm issues were involved (Wilkening and Bharadwaj, 1967, 1968; Sawer, 1973). Wilkening and Bharadwaj (1967, 1968) delineated factors for decision making that discriminate between farm resource decisions and farm operations decisions. Joint decision making between husband and wife was more prevalent in farm resource decisions, including purchasing and renting land, borrowing money, and buying major farm equipment or a car. Husbands were more likely to make the decisions themselves concerning farm operations, such as whether to buy fertilizer, what crops to plant, and what brand of machinery to buy.

In their study comparing decision making in families at different points along the rural-urban continuum, Burchinal and Bauder (1965) reported that former semipatriarchal norms have given way to relatively equalitarian norms regardless of place of residence. However, since they were comparing farm families with nonfarm families, decisions concerning the farming operation are not included. This study suggests that egalitarian decision making occurs in the household, but the patriarchal character of the farm operation was not investigated.

The other major decision-making issue is the relation between the woman's involvement in decisions and the success of the farm operation. Beers (1937) reported that as farms became larger and more commercialized, husbands tended to take sole responsibility for farm decisions. Approximately thirty-five years later, Sawer found joint decision making more likely to occur at low income levels. According to Sawer, "As income and farm size increase, [a woman's] opportunities to participate in the management of a large, complex business may be restricted by her limited knowledge and experience" (1973:420). However, Wilkening (1958) suggested that a curvilinear relationship exists between farm income and wife's participation in decision making. According to his study, joint decision making is more likely to occur among middle-income farm families than low- and high-income farm families. In speculating on the reasons for a curvilinear relationship, Straus suggested that at the low-income level fewer managerial decisions are made; consequently, there is less need for the wife to participate. On the other hand, for high-income farmers, "technological complexity, perhaps beyond the wife's knowledge or skill, apparently attenuates the possibilities for the wife to make a useful managerial contribution" (1960:225).

Several authors have noted the limitations of questionnaires in determining who makes decisions in families. Kenkel and Hoffman (1956) found that couples were not accurate in reporting or predicting their respective roles in decision making. In comparing responses of husbands and wives as to who made decisions on twenty-three issues, Wilkening and Morrison (1963) found that the husband and wife agreed only about half of the time. Therefore, Wilkening and Morrison suggested that findings of the decision-making studies of farm families must be interpreted with caution. There is some indication that respondents answer who "ought" to make decisions rather than who actually makes them.

Straus (1958, 1960), Blood (1958), and Sawer (1973) all explored the sexual division of labor on the family farm. In two studies, Straus (1958, 1960) examined the differences between the wives of low-success and high-success farmers. Relying on Parsons' theoretical analysis of the family, Straus (1960) attempted to test whether occupational and technological complexity accentuate role differentiation between husband and wife on the farm. According to Parsons' structural functionalist theory, role differentiation occurs such that the husband emphasizes the adaptive-goal attainment functions while the wife emphasizes integrative-supportive functions. Straus constructed a "wife role supportiveness index" in order to summarize his findings. Due to the nonrepresentativeness of his sample and the "ad hoc nature of the index," he explained that he did not attempt to test the hypothesis that farm operator success is associated with an integrative-supportive wife. Nevertheless, he did conclude that the wife-role factor is helpful in understanding the technological behavior of farm operators. In his earlier study of the wife's role in the settlement of the Columbia River Basin, Straus (1958) concluded that the direct economic contribution of the wife does not make a difference to the success of the farm operation. He suggested that the role of the successful farmer's wife is identical to the role of the successful corporate executive's wife. The differentiating factors between the wives of high- and low-success farmers "seem to be those which enable the wife to play a personally supportive and complementary role in helping her husband meet the many decisions, difficulties, and frustrations which arise in developing a new farm" (1958:64). Interestingly, Straus found significant differences between high- and low-success groups' wives in terms of the percentage who had vegetable gardens and preserved foods. In his study, 83 percent of the high-success group's wives had vegetable gardens compared to 56 percent of the low group. High group wives preserved an average of 350 quarts of food per year, compared to 67 quarts for the low group. Straus discounted the possibility that this work was economically advantageous to women's families. Rather, he emphasized the irrationality of women with a high income engaging in extensive home gardening and canning and went on to suggest that these women were most likely performing these tasks to fulfill the traditional farm wife role. In both studies, he concluded that the work of the wife is not correlated with the success of the farming operation.

Sawer (1973) agreed with Straus concerning the relationship between technological change and the woman's role on the farm. She says, "There is an indication that the husband's acceptance of technological change is associated with his wife's assuming a supporting role defined as homemaker and mother" (1973:421). In discussing the implications of her study, Sawer concluded that wives of financially successful farmers should not be encouraged by extension services to participate in farm decisions.

Blood (1958), on the other hand, did not discount the farm wife's economic contribution to the farm operation. In comparing the work of urban and farm women, Blood emphasized that farm women work much harder than urban women. "Farm wives not only take over from their husbands a substantial share of household tasks and from commercial enterprises a large proportion of consumer goods production but they also help their husbands with farm work" (1958:172). Blood noted that despite this work, farm wives have no more power in decision making than do urban wives.

Except for Blood's study, the studies on decision making and sexual division of labor on family farms assume that the primary contribution that women make on farms is noneconomic. Even when women's subsistence production is noted, it is underappreciated. Witness Straus's 1958 description of women's subsistence production as economically "irrational." In all the studies women's role as mother and homemaker is emphasized over their involvement in the farm enterprise.

As has been noted, the findings of the decision-making studies should be interpreted with caution. Reports of who makes decisions that are considered to be in the male realm may be biased such that both husbands and wives report that men make decisions more than they actually do. Despite the theoretical and methodological limitations of these studies, they all conclude that in highly successful farm operations, the role of the woman in farm decisions and tasks is minimized. Thus, there is an indication that market-oriented, high-technology farming excludes women from decision making. As agricultural production increasingly occurs on larger, specialized farms, it might be expected that women will continue to be removed from decisions relating to agricultural production. In order for this trend to be reversed, directed action must be taken to assure women's participation in decisions related to agriculture. Through identifying women who are currently participating in decision making in agriculture, the present study attempts to determine how women are and can be included in decisions relating to agriculture.

Farm Women's Work Today

The work of women on farms today can only be understood within the context of the changing structure of agriculture. The following three factors are of particular importance to women's work: displacement of people from agricultural production; technological changes; and reliance on off-farm work.

Rural people are continually losing their farms. During the twentieth century there has been a tendency toward the

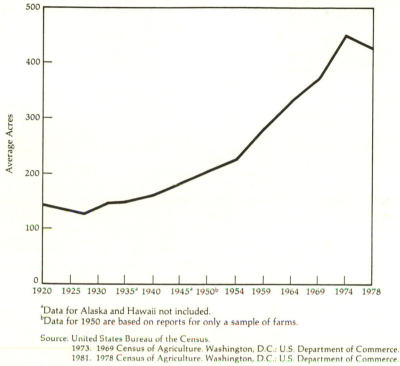

^aData for Alaska and Hawaii not included.
^bData for 1950 are based on reports for only a sample of farms.

Source: United States Bureau of the Census.
    1973. 1969 Census of Agriculture. Washington, D.C.: U.S. Department of Commerce.
    1981. 1978 Census of Agriculture. Washington, D.C.: U.S. Department of Commerce.

Figure 1.1 Average Acreage per Farm, 1920-1978.

concentration of agricultural land. Since the mid-1930s the number of farms has declined dramatically, while the amount of agricultural land has remained relatively constant. The total number of farms has decreased from approximately 7 million in the thirties to 2.5 million in 1978. Thus, from the mid-1930s to the present we see an increase in the average size of farms (Figure 1.1). The concentration of agricultural land has been most dramatic since World War II.

The loss of farms is not evenly distributed across the rural population. Rural people with small farms are more likely to lose their land than are farmers with large landholdings. There has been a continual decrease in the number of farms with fewer than fifty acres since 1935. On the other end of the spectrum, the number of farms with over a thousand

Table 1.1   Distribution of Farmland by Region

Region	Farms of fewer than 50 acres		Farms of more than 1,000 acres	
	Percentage of		Percentage of	
	Owners	Land	Owners	Land
Northeast	66.4	14.9	.2	20.7
North Central	43.5	6.8	.3	23.5
South	69.3	14.3	.4	26.3
Great Plains	35.0	1.8	3.3	23.3
Southwest	77.6	6.3	4.7	67.5
Northwest	72.7	6.3	5.9	60.9

Source: Schertz (1979b:35).

acres increased from 55,000 in 1925 to 162,156 in 1978 (U.S. Bureau of the Census, 1973, 1981). While only 6.6 percent of farm units are over one thousand acres, they currently include 40 percent of the farmland. As can be seen in Table 1.1, the distribution of farmland varies by region. In the United States today, 5 percent of all landowners own more than half of all farmland (Boxley, 1979). Fewer people are farming, on increasingly larger farms.

It is often an economic necessity for farmers to expand their holdings. The survival of the farm is tied to the creation of profit. Large-scale farmers have an advantage over smaller farmers in that they generally have easier access to credit, more capital equipment, more fertilizer, and are able to survive on lower profit margins. Small farmers are increasingly caught in a cost-price squeeze and forced out of business.

Several authors have suggested that there is a transition toward a dual economy in agriculture: larger commercial farms, on the one hand, small farms based on subsistence, retirement, and part-time farming on the other (Carter and Johnson, 1978). The small commercial farmers, who are located between these two groups, are being displaced. The outstanding feature of this dual economy is that many more people are on small farms that are not economically viable than are on the large commercial farms. Schertz (1979a) reports that 1.8 million farms had sales of less than $20,000 in 1978, while only 187,000 had sales exceeding $100,000; and of those farms with over $100,000 in sales, 63,000 had sales exceeding $200,000. While farms with sales of over $200,000 comprised only 2.4 percent of all farms in 1978, they accounted for 39 percent of all sales. The increasing concentration of wealth among farmers is revealed in examining the share of farm receipts received by the 50,000 largest farms over time. In 1960, sales of these farms constituted 23 percent of farm receipts. Their share of sales rose to 30 percent in 1967, and 36 percent in 1978 (Schertz, 1979a). As these farms increased their share of the wealth, farmers on the remainder of the farms became increasingly impoverished.

Certain groups of farmers have suffered more than others. Perhaps the hardest hit are the small black farm operators in the South. The number of southern black farm operators decreased 68 percent between 1959 and 1969 (Bildner, 1974). Many of these farmers were tenants who were forced off the land to make way for larger farmers. With the introduction of technology, such as the mechanical cotton harvester, owners were able to farm more land without relying on tenants. Schwartz (1945) suggests that a major reason for the importance of tenancy in cotton production after the Civil War is that such a mode of land tenure assured plantation owners a pool of resident labor—the tenants' and sharecroppers' wives and children. These women and children were no longer needed with the introduction of mechanical harvesters. The increased concentration of agricultural capital and land forces many of the rural poor to migrate to urban areas in search of jobs. At a time when urban unemployment is already high, the migration of rural blacks to cities only serves to increase the number of people who are out of work. People who are displaced from agriculture often find no means to support themselves.

Both women and men have been displaced from agricultural production. Women who remain on farms continue to be involved in agricultural production. A national survey of 2,059 farm women reports that 55 percent of women considered themselves main operators of their farms (Jones and Rosenfeld, 1981). The survey also reports the extent of women's involvement in farm tasks. Table 1.2 reports the percentage of women either regularly or occasionally involved in various farm tasks. It indicates that women are quite involved in most aspects of agricultural production, including the tasks which have traditionally been considered men's work. Unfortunately there are no national data to compare the involvement of women's work in agriculture over time. A report by Wilkening (1981) on changes in women's involvement in farm tasks in Wisconsin from 1962 to 1979 suggests that women's involvement in farm tasks has increased. The most important shift, according to Wilkening, relates to women's increased responsibility for recordkeeping and obtaining information about farm matters.

The concentration in agricultural production has been accompanied by transformations in agricultural techniques. Technological developments in agriculture have benefited large-scale farmers and allowed the possibility of even larger farms. The impact of the changes in technology on the role of women in agriculture has been explored in developing countries (Boserup, 1970), but seldom in the United States.

THE BROILER INDUSTRY

The nature of mechanization and technical control of agricultural production varies by crop and region. Examination of the social and economic impact of mechanization in particular commodities is a method of studying changes in agricultural techniques. Several studies (Friedland and Barton, 1975; Friedland, Barton, and Thomas, 1978) have noted the social impact of mechanization in tomato and lettuce production. In an attempt to assess the impact of technological change in women's work in agriculture, Friedland and Barton's method of focusing on a specific commodity is useful.

Breimyer (1962) has argued that industrialized agriculture is more likely to be found in livestock production than in crop production. Large-scale confinement operations are increasingly characterizing livestock production in the United

Table 1.2 Farm Women's Involvement in Farm and Home Tasks

| | Percentage responding | | | |
	Regular duty	Occa- sionally	Never	N^a
Plowing, disking, cultivating, or planting	11	25	63	(2,257)
Applying fertilizers, herbi- cides, or insecticides	5	12	83	(2,377)
Doing other field work without machinery	17	25	58	(2,281)
Harvesting crops or other products, including run- ning machinery or trucks	22	29	49	(2,351)
Taking care of farm animals, including herding or milk- ing dairy cattle	37	29	34	(1,944)
Running farm errands, such as picking up repair parts or supplies	47	38	15	(2,483)
Making major purchases of farm or ranch supplies and equipment	14	23	63	(2,455)
Marketing products—that is, dealing with wholesale buyers or selling directly to consumers	15	18	67	(2,380)
Bookkeeping, maintaining records, paying bills, or preparing tax forms for the operation	61	17	22	(2,489)
Doing household tasks like preparing meals, house- cleaning, and so on	97	2	1	(2,499)
Supervising the farm work of other family members	24	26	50	(2,060)
Supervising the work of hired farm labor	11	25	64	(1,643)
Taking care of a vegetable garden or animals for family consumption	74	14	12	(2,350)
Looking after children	74	13	13	(1,846)
Working on a family or in- home business other than farm or ranch work	34	13	53	(1,139)

^{a}Total excludes those who say task was "not done" on their operation.
Source: Jones and Rosenfeld (1981:18).

States. Confinement operations, which are used for cattle, hogs, and chickens, attempt to apply the techniques of industrial production to agriculture. Focusing on technological transformations in broiler production helps us understand the changes in women's work. The care of poultry has historically been women's work, and the broiler industry has led the way in transforming the techniques of agricultural production. The example reveals how the industrialization of production transforms women's work. Also, by focusing on the broiler industry, which is often held up as an ideal for the production of livestock (Walsh notes that "the broiler industry . . . is as close to applying the mass production techniques of industry as any sector of agriculture" [1975:31]), possible future impacts of changes in agricultural techniques may be considered.

In the 1920s, chickens were produced on thousands of family farms, where eggs were hatched, feed was grown, and the chickens were often slaughtered and dressed. Women were usually responsible for the care of chickens. During that period, research on improving the production of chickens abounded and radically altered the production processes. The production of poultry indoors without sunshine became possible because of research on various properties of vitamin D. Thus, chickens began to be raised indoors in large chicken houses. In addition to altering the environment in which chickens were raised, research actually changed the nature of the chicken itself. As Talbot describes scientific research on chickens: "General purpose breeds were crossed and recrossed, all the while searching for the 'chicken of tomorrow,' broad breasted with thick drumsticks" (1978:4–5). The major purpose of the research was to improve production efficiency. Thus, researchers attempted to grow their "new" chicken at the fastest speed and the lowest cost. Feed formulas were introduced, and chickens are now continually fed antibiotics to fend off disease. Research has allowed for increased output by improving the feed conversion ratio. In 1925, a 3.5-pound bird could be raised in sixteen weeks with 12 pounds of feed. By 1968, a 3-pound bird could be raised in half the time with 6.8 pounds of feed.

Today, chickens are raised in controlled environments, where the temperature, light, and food are all strictly regulated in accordance with scientific knowledge concerning production efficiency. The technical manipulation of chickens is accompanied by changes in the means of production. Prior to the industrialization of poultry production, the farmer raised food for the chickens. The farmer usually owned the farm, made decisions about what to produce and how to produce it, and was responsible for the care of chickens. (On nonspecialized family farms, women were usually responsible for the care of chickens.) As late as 1950, 28 percent of all chickens produced in the United States were consumed by the farm household; by 1971, only 7 percent of chickens were consumed on the farm on which they were raised (USDA, 1972). Thus, if it is assumed that women had the major responsibility for raising chickens for nonmarket uses, it seems that a substantial amount of women's agricultural labor was displaced in a twenty-one-year period.

Specialization and concentration in chicken production appeared in the 1930s, such that firms specialized in breeding, hatching, feed milling, processing, or marketing (Talbot, 1978). With the industrialization of poultry production, both the women and the men of the farm lost control of production decisions. Not only have many small farmers discontinued raising chickens for subsistence, but even the independent chicken grower has disappeared. Today, approximately 90 percent of broiler growers are under contract with corporations (USDA, 1972). At the present time, broilers are typically raised on specialized farms, where the farmer owns the land and buildings while a corporation owns the chickens, provides feed and pharmaceuticals, and makes management decisions. The corporations have field staff experts in chicken raising and management who instruct the farmers (Walsh, 1975). In fact, a Congressional Committee on Small Business Problems in the Poultry Industry reported in 1963 that "contract production arrangements and vertical integration have definitely tended toward making the grower a mere hired hand" (Talbot, 1975:6). Thus, while family owns the land, they do not necessarily control the farming operation. And surely the rural women who once handled poultry production have little place in decision making.

OFF-FARM LABOR

As costs rise faster than prices, farm producers are faced with a decline in income. As a consequence, many farm families have lost their land and have been forced to move to urban areas. An alternative to selling the farm and moving to the city is the selling of labor. In 1978, all farm families combined received 56 percent of their income from off-farm sources. Families on smaller farms are more likely to rely on off-farm sources. On farms with sales of less than five thousand annually, 90 percent of family income is from off-farm sources (USDA, 1979). The adoption of an off-farm work pattern is a direct result of low income and is an option that is pursued when all others fail (Hedley, 1976).

The type of off-farm work pattern that is adopted depends on the labor opportunities in the area, the labor requirements on the farm and in the home, the differential between women's and men's wages, the stage of the family life cycle, and the success of the farm operation. Studies of part-time farming are usually based solely on the type of work performed by men (Coughenour, 1980; Loomis, 1965; Fugitt et al., 1977; Frauendorfer, 1966). These studies ignore or undervalue the economic value of the work performed by women on the farm and in the labor force. One alternative of a household in response to economic pressure is for men to work off the farm. Coughenour (1980) reports that in 1974, 55 percent of all farmers were part-time farmers. When the man works off the farm, the woman often assumes a major portion of the responsibility for the operation of the farm (Lyson, 1979). Gladwin (1982) reports that a woman will often quit a low-paying off-farm job to farm full time when her husband takes a full-time off-farm job. The increasingly high incidence of men working off the farm on limited-resource farms suggests that women are doing a larger share of the work and making more decisions on these farms.

Another option of farm households dealing with limited

farm income is the employment of women off the farm. If the woman works off the farm, the man is defined as a full-time farmer, although the labor of the woman on the farm is substantially reduced. Part-time-farming studies have rarely considered the impact on the male's work role when the woman enters the nonfarm labor force. In her study of Florida farms, Gladwin (1982) found that women are most likely to work full time off the farm if they have high education, high earnings potential, and a babysitter for their children. Women who work full time off the farm do little or no farming. Men whose wives work off the farm have access to additional income that may enable them to continue to work full-time on the farm. With the exception of Gladwin's study, the employment of rural women has not been studied as a factor affecting the farming capabilities of males.

With the increase in rural industrialization and the economic difficulties of farming, more farm women are entering the labor force (Sweet, 1972). A recent study of farm women in Kentucky revealed that 38 percent of farm women were employed off the farm (Bokemeier, Keith, and Sachs, 1980). As Boulding suggests, "Women will be caught in a triple squeeze. Not only do they have to fill in for their part-time farming husbands on the land, but they themselves are increasingly entering the nonfarm labor force . . . and must moonlight their own farm work (1980:262).

Regardless of whether women reside in rural or urban areas, they are generally employed in a labor market distinct from the male labor market (Oppenheimer, 1970). Employed women are concentrated in low-wage industries and occupations. From the advent of the factory system in the United States to the present time, specific jobs were designed primarily for women. Recent efforts at rural industrialization, particularly in the South, have frequently looked to rural women for a cheap supply of labor. Expansion of the service sector of the economy has also relied on the employment of women at low-wage levels. Women on farms often enter the paid labor force in menial, low-paying jobs. In contrast to the single, young, rural women who worked in factories at the beginnings of industrialization, many of the women working in factories today are married. Similar to the situation of women at the advent of industrialization, it appears that women now working in factories may be earning wages not as independent income but as an additional source of income for the maintenance of the farm operation.

The contribution of women's unpaid and paid labor to farm operations has not been adequately investigated, although from the literature, there is some indication that women's work on limited-resource farms is quite substantial, and Galarza (1977) reports that women are increasingly being employed as farm workers on large commercial farms. While women are contributing labor to agricultural production, their role in management and decision making, especially on large-scale farms, has not kept pace with their labor contribution. Women seem to be more involved in decision making on limited-resource farms, but agricultural production is increasingly being performed on large-scale farms. On these farms, women tend to be only minimally involved in decision making and are often relegated to performing agricultural labor.

2

Domesticity

Women's work on farms is defined by the sexual division of labor in society as well as historical transformations in the structure of agriculture. Women on farms are involved in various types of labor including agricultural production, domestic production, and off-farm work. On farms, as throughout society, a distinction exists between men's work and women's work. The domestic ideology provides legitimation for the division of labor between men and women and the subordinate position of women. The keystone of this ideology is the notion that women are domestic beings. The purpose of this chapter is to examine the interplay between the domestic and agricultural work of farm women and the ideology in the United States that emphasizes the primacy of women's domestic role. Factors that will be examined include the emergence of domestic ideology in the United States, the adoption of domesticity by women of different classes, the legitimation of domesticity through religion and science, and the effect of government promotion of a domestic ideology for rural women.

Over time there has been an increasing emphasis on domestic work as the proper realm for farm women. While the farm did not undergo the spatial separation of work from home that occurred in cities, the sexual division of labor on the farm changed not altogether differently than in the cities. As with middle-class urban women, the middle-class farm woman's role was increasingly limited to the domestic realm. A 1912 report published by the USDA describes this transition in a section entitled "Reduction of Women's Work to Domestic Affairs." As the report states,

> The outdoor work of white women on the farms of medium and better sort has very greatly declined from early days, and the decline was more especially marked after the Civil War. Farmers' wives and daughters no longer milk the cows and work in the field and care for the livestock. They do not work in the kitchen garden as much as before, nor assist so much in fruit and hay harvest; they are making less butter, and cheese making on the farm has become a lost art. They may care for the poultry and the bees, do housework and gather vegetables for the table, and cook and keep the dwelling in order. Their domestic work is substantially the limit of their work on the farm. [Holmes, 1912a:29]

There is some question about how widespread this change was among farm women, but there was certainly a transition occurring in the work that well-to-do women performed. According to this report, women were increasingly eliminated from tasks that took them outside the farm home. As in the industrialized urban sector, women were relegated to tasks in the home while men worked outside of the home. The type of domestic work performed by women on farms varied from that of urban women in that farm families often raised their own food, with women responsible for growing, processing, and preserving subsistence crops.

The increasing commercialization of agricultural production influenced farm women's work in two ways. On the one hand, as production occurred for the purpose of selling goods on the market, women were likely to be eliminated from the labor process. According to Ankarloo (1979), market-oriented farming perfers male to female labor. On the other hand, goods that women had previously produced in the home such as butter and cheese were increasingly being manufactured by commercial firms outside the home. The commercialization of food production displaced women from work they previously performed.

The Nature of Domestic Labor

To understand the assignment of domestic work to women, it is essential to know the nature of domestic labor. Daly (1978) has suggested that in order to explore women's subordination it is necessary to examine the etymology of everyday language. She explains that deceptive perceptions about women have been implanted through language. "Deception is embedded in the very texture of the words we use" (1978:3). Although the dictionary definition of *domestic* is not directly translated into the reality of women's experience, it is interesting to examine the etymology of the word. The first definition of *domestic* that is given in *The Oxford English Dictionary* is "having the character or position of the inmate of a house; housed." The use of the words *inmate* and *housed* in this definition clearly reveals that domestic labor is forced upon the worker by others. The major focus is on confinement. Other applicable definitions include: "of or belonging to the home, house, or household," "native, homegrown, homemade," and "not nomad or wild." Thus, while domestic labor could be defined simply as work done in the home, the primary meaning of *domestic* implies forced confinement or lack of freedom. Women's domestic duties do not simply involve work that must be done in the home, but seem to imply confinement to the home.

Capitalist production has resulted in a spatial separation of domestic work from other types of production. Domestic labor is organized differently from labor involved in the production of surplus value. Women are not paid for their work in either wages or salaries. Dahl and Snare suggest that the housewife is in a "quasi-feudal work arrangement outside the money economy" (1978:17). In fact, they compare the work situation of the housewife to the houseman of the past. In both of these situations, the working hours are not stipulated, but the worker is expected to always be "on call," the worker is paid in goods rather than money, and the payment varies according to the status of the employer rather than as a function of the job performed.

The transference of production from the home to factories resulted in a separation of the home and the work place. The family unit was no longer the unit of production. The breaking up of the family as the unit of production occurred differently across different classes. While women of the rising bourgeoisie were expected to adhere to the tenets of domestic ideology, lower-class women were expected to enter the factories. In fact, the initial transference of production from the home to the factory occurred in textiles, a field that was traditionally women's work. Women followed their cotton to the factories. The development of the textile industry relied on female labor and therefore occurred without removing men's labor from the fields.

At the time that agriculture was the most important type of production, men remained working in the agricultural sphere while women were sent to factories. Women's labor was viewed as less important than men's. Women were used as an available supply of cheap labor during the initial phases of industrialization in this country. As Hartmann explains the progress of industrialization,

> In the process, women, children, and men in rural areas all suffered dislocation and disruption, but they experienced this in different ways. Women forced into unemployment by the capitalization of agriculture more frequently than men, were more available to labor, both in the domestic putting-out system and in the early factories. It is often argued both that men resisted going into the factories because they did not want to lose their independence and that women and children were more docile and malleable. [1976:149]

As manufacturing rapidly expanded and began to be the basis of American economic growth, men were brought into the industrial labor force. Throughout the twentieth century, except during the thirties, economic pressures have forced both men and women to leave the farm to form the urban labor pool. Workers were needed in industrial production rather than agricultural production.

The transition to an industrialized, urbanized society was by no means easy. The reorganization of production was accompanied by an upheaval of the morality and ethics of rural life. Women were called upon to mediate and soften this upheaval through providing a moral and ethical home life.

Capitalism and the Emergence of Domestic Ideology

The bourgeois way of life involved a recodification of ideas about women. Central to this challenge was the emphasis on women as domestic beings (Hall, 1979). With the intro-duction of capitalist production, spheres of labor are separated between the home and the factories. Middle-class women's work is in the home, while men work for wages outside the home. As this process occurred in the late eighteenth and nineteenth centuries, the household became the basis for proper religious and moral lives. Capitalist relations were clearly perceived by the upper classes to be based on ex-ploitation of labor. Although morality and religion were not the basis of capitalist relations of production, the upper classes were not in favor of abandoning morality and religion entirely. Morality and religion were assigned to the home, a sphere separate from the exploitative relations in the outside world. The outside world was defined as hostile, while the home was the bastion of affection and morality (Hall, 1979). Since middle-class married women worked in the home, they were expected to uphold morality. Domesticity was equated with morality.

The ideology that woman's place is in the home serves the interests of both capitalism and male domination. The reverence for the home and women's position therein occurred at a time in which traditional patriarchal authority in the home was being undercut by industrialization. As Ewen writes, "While the cultivation of the home was always spoken of with reverence for the family, it was in fact characterized by the shift of authority away from the family" (1976:136). As production continually shifted from the home to industry, the authority of the home was challenged by the authority of industry. Ewen points out that the rise in social production offered the possibility of overcoming patriarchal control. Emphasizing the dialectical nature of industrialization, Ewen notes that although labor was exploited under the implementation of the wage system, the wage system provided the possibility of democratizing the relations between men and women. However, the industrialists were able to harbor elements of patriarchal authority that could be used for the benefit of their interests. According to Ewen, "The decline of pre-industrial patriarchy had been integral to industrial ascendency, yet the adaptation of Victorian family ideology to the commodity context seemed integral to the maintenance of a reconstituted patriarchy" (1976:129).

Despite the fact that production was leaving the home, the notion that women's place was in the home persisted. Capitalism was served in three ways through the removal of production from the home and the continuation of domestic ideology: the creation of surplus value; the supply of a reserve labor force; and increased consumption.

As capitalism expanded, it was necessary to expand the types of commodities it produced. Braverman explains the process by which the commodification of goods and services proceeds: "In the period of monopoly capitalism, the first step in the creation of the universal market is the conquest of all goods production by the commodity form, the second step is the conquest of increasing range of services and their conversion into commodities, and the third step is a "product cycle" which invests new products and services, some of which become indispensable as the conditions of modern life change to destroy alternatives" (1974:281).

The creation of this universal market has occurred through the continual absorption of the unpaid labor which women once performed in the home into the marketplace. The home production of food, clothing, and numerous other household goods was gradually transferred to the factory. In addition, services such as nursing, education, and care of the elderly, which women typically performed, have switched to the marketplace. Women often follow their work to factories, or perform service jobs in restaurants, hospitals, and hotels. When their labor is performed in the marketplace, surplus value is created and capital is enriched.

Women have continuously been employed outside the home despite the maintenance of the domestic ideology. Many women were drawn into the paid labor force as the wages of an adult male were inadequate to support the family. In other cases, no male was present, or the male could not find employment. "The notion that a woman's place is in the home acted to create an ambivalence among working mothers: it served as an ideological justification for the occasional entry and exit of women into and out of industry" (Ewen, 1976:118).

The domestic ideology has provided the legitimation for maintaining women as a reserve labor force. When the demands of capital are such that women laborers are needed, they can be hired. As the labor market shrinks, women can return home to their proper place without creating "unemployment."

In addition, the ideology that emphasizes the primacy of women's domestic role justifies the sexual segregation of labor in the marketplace. Women are employed in low-wage industries and occupations that are frequently nonunionized. When women's major roles are defined as relating to motherhood and the home, their wages and job opportunities are viewed as secondary. The exploitation of women workers on the job and their confinement to low-wage positions are overlooked by both women and men as they adhere to domestic ideology.

Woman's place might be in the home, according to domestic ideology, but the home was continually becoming a different place (Ewen, 1976). Traditional productive activities left the home, thereby changing women's role to that of consumer. As women's productive activities were transferred to industry, women increasingly confronted the necessity of buying goods. The products of home labor were uneconomic compared to the cheaper manufactured goods produced by wage labor.

In addition to the economic aspect, advertisers and the educational system managed to "turn 'homemade' into a derogation and 'factory-made' or 'storebought' into a boast" (Braverman, 1974:276).

As industry expanded production, it was also faced with the necessity of increasing consumption. The culture emphasized that industry (production) was the world of men, and therefore women were to be the consumers (Ewen, 1976). In his study of advertising in the 1920s, Ewen found that ads appealed to women, emphasizing the importance of their consumer role. The notion that women were the "managers of the home" because they purchased the goods to be used at home was touted by industry. Participation in consumption does not imply control or self-determination, however. Advertisements suggested that a woman's role as consumer offered her a liberated existence, since she had free choice of innumerable goods. They often suggested that women's traditional way of working was based on superstitions, while the corporations had scientific knowledge. Thus, women were encouraged to rely on corporate authority in making consumption decisions. Advertisers also appealed to the contradictions that women experienced as their productive activities left the home. Motherhood remained and had become the primary duty of women in the home. Ewen explains that women were told that various commodities could solve their problems with motherhood. If women purchased the proper goods, their children would be successful. Ads played on the mother's guilt at not being perfect mothers. "Through consumption, the ads argued, the broad crisis of mothers in industrial America could be resolved" (Ewen, 1976:174). Industry continually created more and more needs, and women were appealed to in order to consume the goods that industry produced.

Thus, in many ways, the perpetuation of domestic ideology served the interests of an expanding capitalist economy. The continual shift away from family authority threatened to undermine patriarchal authority, but patriarchal authority continued under different forms in industrial society.

Others have attempted to analyze the value of domestic labor under capitalism. Similar to domestic scientists, these authors attempt to give meaning to women's work in the face of the domestic void. Weir and Wilson (1973) assert that women's productive function occurs within the realm of reproduction of the conditions of production. This includes both the reproduction of labor power and the reproduction of relations of production. Women are crucial in the reproduction of labor power in that they have the major responsibility for the reproduction of children. Gerstein (1973) understands domestic work as the production and maintenance of labor power. He suggests that the work done within the family to care for and maintain its members is at the same time the maintenance of their ability to labor. Since labor power is a commodity, the production and maintenance of labor power is a form of commodity production.

Another dimension of the production function of the domestic realm is the reproduction of wage labor. The reproduction of wage labor is brought about through consumption, and women have the primary responsibility for using wages. Vogel (1973) suggests that women are engaged in productive activity through the expenditure of the wage. Thus, according to these studies, domestic work is productive activity in a capitalist system. The main purpose of these studies is to prove that women's domestic work is productive although they no longer produce goods in the home.

While women's domestic work does reproduce labor, these analyses often overlook the fact that the men in each household benefit from women's assumption of the domestic role. In fact, Gardiner (1975) criticizes Secombe's (1973) interpretation of domestic labor for its failure to recognize the sexist nature of the relations between working-class men and women. She also notes that Secombe attempts to integrate domestic labor into Marx's theory of value, whereas a more radical reinterpretation of domestic labor from a feminist perspective might be more revealing. Women perform domestic labor not only because it serves the interest of capital, but also because it serves men in each household.

Science and Domesticity

While the relegation of women to domestic labor was initially legitimated through appeals to morality and religion, science gradually replaced religion as the legitimation of women's confinement to domestic work. The way science provides legitimation for the division of labor between men and women is particularly apparent in agriculture. Strasser (1978) suggests that the transition of the home from a production unit to a consumption unit was accomplished by the beginning of the twentieth century. While Strasser is correct with respect to the urban household, the agriculturally based home continued to be a production unit beyond the turn of the century. Even within this production unit, however, science supported a sexual division of labor that assigned women to domestic work.

Science began to influence the rural way of life directly in the United States in the late nineteenth century. In 1862, the Morrill Act paved the way for the establishment of land grant colleges in every state. Agricultural experiment stations existed in most states by the early twentieth century, and the Extension Service was established in 1914 for the purpose of communicating scientific information to farmers. The agricultural science establishment was funded by federal and state governments.

In this government-supported agricultural science establishment, the "natural" sexual division of labor remained unquestioned, and consequently agricultural science became a male field and domestic science a female field. Male extension agents distributed scientific knowlege of agriculture to male farmers and female extension agents taught domestic science to women on farms. This division was not one of equality, since agriculture was certainly viewed as far more important than domestic science by university administrators. As Margaret Mead noted, "The historic tendency of males to regard their activities (usually extradomestic) as more important than those of females was thus accentuated when the roles of men and women on the farm were professionalized" (1976:10). The roots of domestic science and agricultural science are not identical, but each set out to transform and legitimate the practice of their respective fields. Domestic science was directed toward both rural and urban women, while agricultural science was directed primarily toward rural men. In order to comprehend why agricultural science was directed toward men and domestic science toward women, it is necessary to critically examine the establishment of these sciences.

Science, in the name of neutrality, often legitimates various technological and societal changes. The application of science to agriculture has radically altered the practice of farming and the rural social structure. At the outset, agricultural science was hailed as progressive. Its main order of business was to increase productivity and encourage the commercialization of farming. Agricultural science was not directed toward the subsistence farmer, but favored large commercial farmers.

The formation of a government-supported scientific and educational establishment for agriculture has been described by McConnell (1953) as an effort to reduce rural discontent. The Populist movement of the 1890s was composed largely of farmers demanding radical social and economic change. Agricultural colleges, experiment stations, and extension services were the "positive alternatives" which the government established to ease the mounting tensions between the Populists and bankers and businessmen (Busch and Lacy, 1981; McConnell, 1953).

Agricultural science also supported the "natural" sexual division of labor. Degler provides evidence from the late nineteenth and twentieth centuries, "suggesting that when a farmer could afford to keep his wife out of the field work he did so" (1980:406). Smuts (1971) also notes that heavy field work was taken over by men on farms which became prosperous. It is not surprising that as agricultural science favored the wealthy male farmers, women were increasingly displaced from agricultural production. The situation of women who were involved in field work should not be romanticized. These women were often the poorest, performing both field work and the work around the farm home that all women were expected to perform. The point is that men usually decided what work the women would perform. When extra help could be hired, women left the fields for the home. In the early years of the twentieth century, science began to address women's work in the home, signaling the rise of domestic science.

In the early nineteenth century, religion legitimated the cult of domesticity, but by the 1890s science attempted to pick up where religion left off. The emphasis on preserving the home came at a time when many Americans felt the traditional home was in danger of disappearing. Women were increasingly voicing discontent about their confinement to the domestic realm. The women's movement was particularly strong; in addition to the movement for suffrage, women were demanding numerous economic and social changes that would benefit them. Thus, while agricultural science was established during a period of rural unrest, domestic science was established at a time when organized discontent among women was gaining momentum. In fact, neither of these sciences was a neutral force. Both were used to guide social change in a particular direction.

Women attempted to establish domestic science from the late 1890s to 1910. Ellen Swallow Richards led the way in promoting a scientific approach to basic household tasks. Ehrenreich and English (1978) explain the emergence of domestic science as an attempt to fill the newly created domestic void and thus preserve the home. As more and more of the goods that women had produced at home were produced in factories, middle-class women had less work to perform in the home. Women were expected to remain in the home despite the fact that most of the productive activities they had performed in the home were transferred to the marketplace.

Science provided a justification for the importance of domestic work. Although many productive tasks were no longer performed in the home, basic tasks such as cleaning remained. The germ theory of disease, which was well known to the public in the 1890s, provided a scientific basis for cleaning. The duties of the housewife from this point included responsibility for public health. As Ehrenreich and English state,

"Here at last was a challenge suitable to the energy and ability of educated women" (1978:143). An appeal to religion no longer convinced middle-class women of the value of a domestic orientation, but science provided a worthy legitimation of domesticity.

Through providing a scientific approach to housework, domestic scientists hoped to provide "meaningful" work for women. As a teacher of home economics at the University of Minnesota noted, "The application of science to matters of common experience give a new meaning to cleaning the wringer, precautions for preserving colors and safeguarding fabrics, washing with gasoline and other operations" (Shepperd, 1909:154). While some women were voicing their protests against their confinement in the home, others were seeking to make their time in the home more meaningful. Science provided the key to meaning. The domestic scientists hoped to raise the status of homemaking through revealing the scientific nature of the work.

Men did not take the scientific part of domestic science seriously. At the first meeting of the American Home Economics Association several men spoke of the importance of home economics. The scientific part of the work was downplayed. As Dr. Elmer Brown, Commissioner of Education of the United States, said in his address to the meeting, "I do not think that in reaching out for the things that are larger and better and more significant, you should forget the fact that the simple work in good cookery and in home hygiene, that constitutes no small part of your interests, is of tremendous consequence for our American home." He went on to say that the "really great significance of your work, after all, is moral" (Journal of Home Economics, 1909:27).

A woman discussing the acceptance of domestic science in New York City schools explained, "It has won approval on its merit as a moral factor in education. Even to the officials in immediate charge of courses of study, an appeal upon a scientific basis seldom succeeds. . . . That it finds favor upon a moral basis is shown in many ways" (Williams, 1909:78). She claimed that it did not matter that school officials failed to recognize the scientific part of their work, as long as they allowed scientifically trained teachers to teach. Her hope was that the scientific nature of domestic science would soon win approval. Today, we can see that her dream never came true.

Men were glad to support women who wanted to teach other women the moral value of staying in the home. At no time did these men take seriously the scientific claim of the scientists, however. This is currently reflected in the low status of home economists relative to other scientists and economists. As Margaret Mead (1976) suggested, men see their work as more important than women's work whether or not women are doing their work in a scientific manner.

Other sciences were supported partially because of the promise of creating commodities and profit. Women recognized that the growth of domestic science was slow because there was no commercial force behind it. As LeBosquet, a domestic scientist, stated, "There are no commercial interests to profit by the extension of home economics education—only the homes of America. The homemakers of America are a tremendous force, however, and often this force can be exerted most effectively through the Women's Clubs" (1909:181).

While this new twentieth-century domesticity was lauded because of its scientific nature, the appeal of domesticity remained a moral one, as it had been in the nineteenth century. The home was juxtaposed to the competitiveness in capitalist society. The fear that the home itself would succumb to the immorality characteristic of capitalism continued from the nineteenth to the twentieth century. The threat to the home came both from outside and within. On the one hand, capitalism posed a threat to the home through transference of numerous domestic tasks to private industry. Margaret Reid described the commercialization of domestic production: "The decrease in household production is written in the development of bakeries, restaurants, power laundries, day nurseries, clothing factories, and even in flourishing beauty parlors" (1934:54). Businessmen saw the home as a marketplace for goods and services. Ellen Richards, the originator of domestic science, voiced her concern of the intrusion of capitalism into the home: "The family home in which every inmate has a share is fast disappearing, selfishness rules from prince to pauper. The inventor who can induce a quarter of the housewives to buy his potato parer makes a huge fortune and one-seventh of the potato goes to the pigs" (*Journal of Home Economics*, 1909:24).

Domestic scientists attempted to save the endangered home through the application of scientific principles to household work (Ehrenreich and English, 1978). A further threat to the home was woman's discontent with her lot. The same class of women were the leaders of both the women's rights movement and the home economics movement. In fact, Ehrenreich and English note that the women's movement was one of the most receptive constituencies of domestic science. These women in the emerging middle classes were not expected to do the same type of domestic production as their mothers. While the extent to which a domestic void actually existed is debatable, it is clear that the more privileged women voiced discontent concerning the importance of their work. The home economists were certainly aware of women's discontent as is evidenced in the description of home economics presented in *The Book of Rural Life*. The description begins, "Modern life possesses so many outside attractions that greater effort than ever before is required of us to maintain a home life that satisfies, appeals and stimulates. Yet no woman, worthy the names of wife and mother, wants to see the home lose its place and influence" (Boyer, 1925:2615). Home economics provided a promise of saving the home by promoting domesticity among women.

Government Support of Domesticity for Rural Women

Another major goal of domestic science was its missionary-type work. Domestic scientists attempted to spread their information to women in the slums and rural women. Ehrenreich and English (1978) describe the establishment of home economics in the urban schools as an effort to discipline and Americanize the urban poor. An emphasis was placed on thrift, orderliness and privacy rather than spontaneity and neighborliness. The spread of domestic science to rural women was undertaken largely through the U.S. Department of Agriculture, which encouraged women to see value in their domestic role. For example, during the early part of the twentieth century, state agricultural experiment stations sent railroad cars to rural areas to demonstrate new developments in scientific farming. The purpose of these trains was to bring the findings of experiment stations to rural areas. In many states, there was one car devoted to agricultural practices and another showing the latest developments in domestic science (Maggard, 1981). These traveling schools encouraged a sexual division of labor that moved women out of agricultural production and into the domestic sphere.

The original orientation of the extension service toward men is described by Elsinger: "Agricultural cooperation (extension) in its inception and early development was viewed largely as a masculine enterprise. Little, if any, effort was made to interest the feminine members of the household. Women were assumed to be directing their efforts into channels better adapted to their talents. Farm business and its resultant profit or loss was considered outside the scope of their proper concern, the home" (1931:5).

The Scientists Today

In the sciences supported by the USDA and the state agricultural experiment stations, a hierarchical sexual division of labor continues. Job segregation by sex pushes women scientists into domestic concerns, while men study agricultural production. The following discussion of the sexual division of labor among publicly funded scientists is based on data obtained through a mail survey of 2,051 agricultural scientists conducted by Lawrence Busch and William Lacy in the summer of 1979. Questionnaires were mailed to a random sample of 2,051 principal investigators listed in the Current Research Information System (CRIS). The names of all persons engaged in research at institutions that receive federal funds for

Table 2.1   Field of Science by Percentage Female and as Percentage of Total Agricultural Scientists

Field	Percentage of total scientists	Percentage female	N
Agronomy	21.3	0.1	(2)
Basic sciences	13.9	3.7	(7)
Animal science	8.4	0.1	(1)
Agricultural economics	8.1	2.5	(1)
Entomology	7.3	4.0	(4)
Plant pathology	6.5	2.2	(2)
Horticulture	6.4	1.1	(1)
Agricultural engineering	5.6	2.5	(2)
Forestry	5.3	0.0	(0)
Environmental science	3.6	5.5	(3)
Nutrition	3.6	32.7	(17)
Food science	3.6	10.2	(5)
Social science	3.3	18.7	(9)
Home economics	0.0[a]	100.0	(3)
Textiles	0.0[a]	66.6	(2)
Other	3.6	4.3	(2)

[a]Less than 0.1 percent.

agriculture are listed on the CRIS file. Due to death, retirement, and several other reasons, 175 questionnaires were excluded from the sample. The corrected sample was 1,876 with 1,431 completed questionnaires returned for a response rate of 76 percent.

Of the 1,431 respondents, 63, or 4.4 percent, were female. Thus, it is apparent that the scientists employed at land grant universities and the USDA are overwhelmingly male. Women scientists who are supported through public agricultural funds are concentrated in nutrition and home economics and are almost totally excluded in fields such as agronomy and animal science. Table 2.1 presents the percentage of the respondents in each discipline and the percentage of women respondents in each discipline. As the table reveals, the fields in which women are concentrated—food science, nutrition, and social science— tend to have a relatively small proportion of the total agricultural scientists. The agricultural sciences with the greatest scientific *man* power—agronomy, animal science, and agricultural economics—are those with the smallest percentage of women.

The focus of agricultural science is clearly on production agriculture. As Margaret Mead noted, this focus on "agricultural production has tended to obscure the need for far more attention to the problems of the preservation, distribution and nutritional value of food" (1976:9). Women's work in agricultural science is primarily in those fields which are overshadowed by production agriculture. The male tendency to undervalue women's work has disastrous consequences for society when the work that is undervaled is research on food preservation, food distribution and nutrition.

Data from the survey allows the possibility of examining the differential between female and male agricultural scientists' concern with consumer issues. Scientists were asked to indicate on a seven-point scale the degree to which their research reflected consumer issues (for example, nutrition). Unfortunately, the small number of women in the sample is problematic in terms of statistical inference. Therefore, the statistics must be interpreted with this limitation in mind.

Women are more likely to be in those disciplines which are concerned with nutrition, but the question must be raised as to whether women maintain a concern with nutrition regardless of their field of science. Since scientific disciplines vary in terms of focus on nutrition, the differences between women and men were examined while simultaneously controlling on the discipline of the scientists. Table 2.2 presents the mean scores and standard deviations for males and females in each field of science on the degree to which their research reflects issues such as nutrition. In the majority of disciplines, women's research is more likely to reflect consumer interest than is men's research. Table 2.2 shows the results of an analysis of variance. Both sex and field of science are significant determinants of interest in consumer issues. The interaction effect is not significant. Thus, regardless of field of science, women are more likely than men to do research that reflects a concern with nutrition. Even in those fields of science which *are* production oriented, women maintain a concern

Table 2.2 Degree to Which Research Reflects Consumer Issues by Sex and Field of Science

Field	Female		Male	
	Mean	S.D.	Mean	S.D.
Agricultural economics	1.00	0.00	2.80	1.95
Agricultural engineering	7.00	0.00	2.07	1.38
Agronomy	4.00	0.00	3.05	1.94
Animal science	——	——	3.89	2.14
Basic science	3.50	2.95	3.00	2.10
Entomology	4.50	2.08	3.07	1.97
Food science	5.20	1.64	5.54	1.47
Forestry	——	——	2.35	1.72
Horticulture	5.00	0.00	3.41	1.98
Nutrition	6.75	0.75	5.26	2.13
Plant pathology	3.00	2.83	2.91	2.02
Environmental science	3.50	2.52	2.53	1.95
Social science	3.88	2.42	2.91	2.03
Home economics	6.00	1.73	——	——
Textiles	6.00	2.00	7.00	0.00
Other	5.50	1.12	3.23	1.87

Analysis of variance

Source of variation	F
Field of science	11.81[a]
Sex	13.16[a]
Interaction	1.33

[a]Significant at .001.

with nutrition and the consumer. As long as the hierarchical sexual division of labor in agricultural science keeps women in disciplines that focus on the consumer, the distance between production agriculture and nutrition will only widen. Issues and areas that have been defined and carved out by women must not be relegated to low-priority items on the overall agenda of agricultural science.

3

The Family Farm

In the United States agriculture has often been organized as a family enterprise. As Friedmann (1978) notes, the family farm is seen as the natural basis of agricultural production in the United States. The viability of the family farm has increasingly become a concern of farmers, scholars, and policy makers. This concern arises from the fact that the number of family farms has declined dramatically in the last fifty years and the nature of those family farms which do remain has changed.

The Changing Nature
of the Family Farm

The family farm was the basis of the American dream of democracy. As Walsh (1975) recalls, sympathy for the family farm goes back at least to Thomas Jefferson, who believed that landholding and farming were the keys to a working democracy. From Jefferson's perspective, the ideal farmer in the early nineteenth century owned his land, did his own work, was his own boss, and bought and sold as little as possible (Brewster, 1979). Brewster points out that the family farm evolved away from Jefferson's model during the nineteenth century. Farming for the market increased, tenancy expanded, and more outside labor was hired. Nevertheless, prior to World War II, it was "still widely believed that a family farm should support a family and that the family should control the operation's resources" (Brewster, 1979:76).

The family farm as an institution encouraged religion, morality, democracy, and individualism. In addition, it was based on patriarchal authority (Folbre, 1980). Thus, the demise of the family farm poses an ideological threat to the foundation of traditional American values. The government finds itself in a legitimation crisis as its policies force more and more people off the land and one of the basic premises of American democracy begins to disappear.

Many of the recent studies on agriculture in the United States have utilized a political economy approach. Buttel (1980), in an excellent summary of the literature, suggests that the major issue in the political economy of U.S. agriculture is whether capitalist agriculture is increasingly replacing the family farm as the dominant form of agricultural production. On the one hand are scholars who argue that family farms are continually being replaced by capitalist production (deJanvry, 1980; Hedley, 1976). Buttel criticizes these scholars for "asking why there has been such a rapid demise of the family labor farm when a more interesting and enduring question concerns why the family labor can be so persistent in an advanced capitalism dominated by large-scale corporate production" (1980:10).

Buttel's criticism is essentially a reiteration of Kautsky's 1899 position on how to study agriculture. As Kautsky stated in *The Agrarian Question*: "To study the agrarian question according to Marx's method, we should not confine ourselves to the question of the future of small scale farming; on the contrary, we should look for all the changes which agriculture experiences under the domination of capitalist production" (Kautsky, 1976).

Both Buttel (1980) and Hedley (1976) emphasize that the family farm or independent commodity production is historically specific to North America. Independent commodity production is a mode of production in which the ownership, operation, and control of the means of production are in the hands of the producer. Labor is organized through the household rather than through wage labor. Scholars utilizing the political economy approach must tackle the question as to why independent commodity production continues despite theoretical notions that assume agricultural production would be similar to industrial production. Kautsky and Lenin agreed with Marx that internal differentiation of the peasantry would occur, with the richer peasants becoming entrepreneurs and the poorer being expropriated from the land to become workers (Bernier, 1976). According to Kautsky, "At a certain stage of development, capitalist commodity production, that is, the worker ceases to be the owner of his means of production. The capitalist stands opposed to the worker, who has lost his property; the worker can no longer work directly for the consumer; he has to work for the capitalist employer, owner of the means of production, to whom he sells his labour power; he becomes a hired worker" (Kautsky, 1976).

While Kautsky expected the demise of the family farm, he was also aware of the strength of the resistance of small farmers. He noted that under capitalism, agriculture vascillates between concentration—larger farms—and disintegration—peasant resistance. However, from his standpoint, this resistance was conservative and not in the best interest of the peasants. The primary factors that enable the small farmer to stay on the land are underconsumption and overwork by the entire family (Kautsky, 1976). Both Bernier (1976) and Friedland, Furnari, and Pugliese (1980) agree that the low standard of living and exploitation of family labor are factors that explain the viability of the family farm at the present time. Also, the continuation of subsistence production largely performed by women on the family farm allows the family to survive on less cash income.

There are a number of other factors that Kautsky and recent scholars utilizing a political economic approach to agriculture cite for the continuation of the family farm. Kautsky noted that centralization and concentration, which are integral features of industrial capitalism, are more difficult to accomplish in agriculture because land is a major factor of production. Especially in regions where land is divided into small holdings, the advancement of capitalist agriculture is slow. The predominance of capitalist agriculture in the West can largely be explained through land settlement patterns that involved large holdings.

Another factor, which Kautsky mentioned, is that small units are supported by the state in its attempt to slow the disintegration of the middle stratum of society. Bernier (1976) also noted that the maintenance of small holders allows for the preservation of property and the keeping of social peace. The United States government does advance programs to support family farms. As Buttel explains, "The persistence of the family labor farm can perform a very crucial legitimation role, thereby prompting the state apparatus to take actions that are aimed at bolstering the viability of the family labor farm" (1980:14).

Kautsky argued that if small farms survive, it is not because they are more productive than the larger capitalist farms. "The real basis of their survival is the fact that they cease to compete with the large capitalist farms which develop by their side. Far from selling the same commodities as the larger farms, these small holdings are often buyers of these commodities. The one commodity which they do possess in abundance, and which bigger holdings need, is their labor power" (1976:34).

In their analysis of agriculture in the United States, Friedland, Furnari, and Pugliese (1980) suggest that there are two sectors, corporate agriculture and family agriculture, which do not compete with each other. Several recent authors emphasize that family farms "undertake many roles and investments that are not attractive to or suitable for large-scale capital annd hence play a vital role in the reproduction of the mode of production as a whole" (Buttel, 1980:13).

The dominance of industrial capital, Bernier (1976) states, explains the persistence of the independent commodity producer: investment in agriculture has been low because investment in industry has been more profitable. Rather than seeking profits through the establishment of large-scale corporate farms, investment in agriculture takes the form of transfer of value. Industrialists sell the means of production, such as tractors, fertilizer, and seed; industrialists transform agricultural products; and bankers lend money to farmers (Bernier, 1976).

Friedmann (1978) emphasizes the importance of technical conditions and the rise of the world market in the predominance of simple commodity production. She mentions that there were experiments in huge capitalist farms on the North American Plains in the late nineteenth century with the rise of the world wheat market. These farms were short-lived in large part because of the introduction of harvesting equipment that reduced the labor demand on farms. With this machinery farm sizes could be expanded without increasing the number of laborers. The organization of the relations of production through the household rather than through wage labor became the dominant mode of producing wheat for the world market. Of course, as Friedmann (1978) points out, these specialized commodity producers were much different from diversified producers whose major aim was subsistence. Despite the fact that subsistence was no longer the aim of wheat farmers, she notes that the flexibility of personal consumption by household producers was advantageous compared to capitalist farmers.

As Wallerstein (1974) suggests, different modes of organizing labor are best suited to particular types of production in the world capitalist economy. The foregoing analysis explains why labor organized through the household is suited to specific types of agricultural production in the United States. In fact, Buttel suggests that in order to understand the fate of independent commodity production, "there must be more work devoted to the exploitation of unpaid family labor in simple commodity production, both in terms of its historical significance and its apparent decline with the development of U.S. agriculture" (1980:18). In this study, the particular concern is with understanding the exploitation of women's labor on the family farms in the United States.

The debate concerning the demise of the family farm in the United States is conditioned by the ideological force of the notion of the *family* farm. While theorists of the political economy of agriculture have noted the legitimation role of the family farm, few have connected this legitimation with the ideology of the family in the United States. Yet the debate over the demise of the family farm is paralleled by a debate over the future of the family. In order to comprehend fully the ideological appeal of the family farm, it is necessary to turn to recent work on the family in advanced industrial society.

As Rapp emphasizes, "The family is a topic which is ideologically charged" (1978:279). The changing nature of the family under capitalism has been the subject of much sociological study ranging from Parsons (1949) to Lasch (1977). Since the rise of capitalism, there has been continued concern about the family's ability to persist. The family is viewed as the last vestige of care and human kindness in an otherwise hostile world. According to Lasch, "The family found ideological support and justification in the conception of domestic life as an emotional refuge in a cold and competitive society" (1977:6). It is primarily women who have been expected to provide this emotional refuge. The concern of Lasch and many others is that the family no longer provides a "haven in a heartless world."

From Lasch's perspective, the authority in the family has been replaced by state domination of personal life. This domination of the state has occurred primarily for the benefit of the competitive, capitalist society.

Support for the continuity of the nuclear family comes from varied perspectives. Feminist theorists, however, have been critical of the nuclear family and its authority structure. Recent revelations of the extent of violence within families of all classes suggest that the nuclear family is not a haven. Spouse abuse, incest, and child abuse abound in families across all classes.

The family farm is a last vestige of a situation in which the household is not physically separated from production. On the family farm, the family works together. The division of labor is organized through the household and not through wage labor. Farmers feel a certain sense of independence by virtue of the fact that they do not work for wages or salaries and their work place is not organized by other authorities. The ideological appeal of the family farm is thus even more emotionally and romantically charged than the appeal of the family per se. The family farm not only appears to be an emotional sanctuary but also seems to be an escape from the capitalist mode of production.

Like the ideology of the family, however, the ideological appeal of the family farm is rife with contradictions. A major contradiction between the ideal and reality of the family farm is that the family farm is not independent. Farmers must produce for the market, which is often the world market. The prices they receive for their commodities are set by urban financiers. Farmers are also dependent on corporations to provide inputs such as feed, fertilizer, pesticides, and machinery. In addition, the ideal of the family farm as a unit on which the family produces its own subsistence plus a surplus is not descriptive of the actual situation on family farms. As Fite (1978) mentions, the family farm has always varied in size, and the income on these farms has covered the range from stark poverty to high prosperity. At present, 55 percent of men living on farms in the United States work off the farm. Women and older children living in farm households often seek off-farm employment. In 1969, 30 percent of farm women worked off the farm, (U.S. Department of Commerce, 1970). Thus, farms organized through family labor are often forced to send one or more family members into the realm of wage labor. The contradiction of the family farm that is of primary importance in this study, of course, is the subordinate position of women.

Capitalism and Patriarchy

A number of recent writings, including those of Hartmann (1976), Cott ((1977), Ehrenreich and English (1978), and Daly (1978), have used the term *patriarchy* to describe the relation between the sexes. Hartmann defines *patriarchy* "as a set of social relations which has a material base and in which there are hierarchical relations between men, and solidarity among them, which enable them to control women" (1976:138).

Various authors have suggested that the use of the term *patriarchy* is inappropriate to describe the relations between the sexes in a capitalist society. For example, Interrante and Lassar (1979) criticize the use of the term because it is used without an analysis of the specific means by which domination is maintained, resisted, or modified. From Interrante and Lassar's perspective, the term *masculinist*, which was used by Ehrenreich and English (1978), better explains the system of male domination under capitalism. They suggest the use of *masculinist* rather than *patriarchy* because *masculinist* is defined as the specific form of male domination under capitalism, while *patriarchy* glosses over the specific means of domination and resistance.

Others argue that patriarchy occurs across a variety of economic systems and is maintained through the private relationship between men and women. From this perspective, domination in one-to-one relationships between men and women is where inequality is established and then incorporated into the economic and social order (Barry, 1979). Rather than focusing on patriarchy, Barry discusses female sexual slavery. She criticizes feminist analyses that define economic domination as the key means of sexual domination, thus obscuring the recognition that sexual domination is "the first cause of sexual power" (1979:9). Sexual and physical violence against women both in the home and outside it reveal the fundamental basis of male power.

The debate over the term *patriarchy* is central to feminist scholars and activists attempting to understand and resist male domination. On the one hand are those who subscribe to the tenets of socialist-feminism, which suggest that male superiority is maintained for the benefit of capitalism. From this perspective, sexism can only be overcome with the overthrow of capitalism. On the other hand are women known as radical feminists. From this perspective, male domination of women is more fundamental than class domination.

Patriarchy transcends cultures, nations, and historical eras. The fact that patriarchy is pervasive, albeit in different forms, does not suggest that the term *patriarchy* is amorphous, as Interrante and Lassar (1979) contend. Rather, the pervasiveness of patriarchy suggests that male domination takes many different forms and occurs in connection with various modes of production. For the purpose at hand, it is necessary to explore the means by which women's subordination is maintained, resisted, and modified in an advanced capitalist society. Of particular importance is the specific form that male domination assumes on farms in the United States. For this purpose, the term *patriarchy*, using Hartmann's (1976) definition, seems appropriate.

Hartmann's excellent analysis of the relation between capitalism and patriarchy concludes that patriarchy has not been vanquished by capitalism. Men controlled the labor of women and children in the family prior to the development of capitalism, and with the separation of the home and the work place, the problem for men was how to maintain control over the labor of women and children. Hartmann points out that patriarchy continues to operate under capitalism. She argues that job segregation by sex is the major mechanism in capitalist society which maintains women's subordination to men. The division of labor between the sexes is hierarchical both in the home and in the work place. Hartmann describes the connection between capitalism and patriarchy:

> Job segregation by sex, I will argue, is the primary mechanism in capitalist society that maintains the superiority of men over women, because it enforces lower wages for women in the labor market. Low wages keep women dependent on men because they encourage women to marry. Married women must perform domestic chores for their husbands. Men benefit, then, from both higher wages and the domestic division of labor. This domestic division of labor, in turn, acts to weaken women's position in the labor market. Thus, the hierarchical domestic division of labor is perpetuated by the labor market, and vice versa. This process is the present outcome of the continuing interaction of two interlocking systems, capitalism and patriarchy. [1976:139]

The Patriarchal Family Farm

In the United States, the family farm is a last vestige of organizing labor through the household. The household is not completely physically separated from the realm of production, and therefore the public/private split that is characteristic of capitalist society is not a necessary feature of the family farm.

The historical roots of the family farm in the United States are based on patriarchal authority (Folbre, 1980). Even on farms that were not primarily oriented to the market, control of the farms rested with the male head of household. Folbre (1980) describes the different types of patriarchal control over sons as compared to wives and daughters. Sons were usually subjected to their father's control during the early years of their lives, while women and daughters were usually subjected to patriarchal authority throughout their lives.

Folbre's (1980) analysis reveals that patriarchal authority was present on colonial New England farms on which the maintenance of household needs was more important than maximizing profits. As she points out, "The most striking feature of women's role in production was the fact they seldom owned means of production and seldom exercised the legal right to independently control the products of their own labor" (1980:8). When women were married, their property and labor belonged to their husbands.

Although there has been much written concerning the interdependence of women and men on the subsistence farm, this interdependence does not necessarily translate into equality. Historical evidence reveals that there was a fairly rigid sexual division of labor on the early New England farms. Control of women's labor process itself probably rested in the hands of the women. Women prepared food, made clothing, raised children, and manufactured basic household necessities. Little information is available concerning women's role in the fields. The male head of household actually owned the means of production and had authority over household decisions. According to Folbre, the male head of household enforced patriarchal norms that excluded women from the most productive and remunerative forms of work.

With the expansion of urban and world markets, production shifted from production for use to production for the market. In the transition from subsistence production to independent commodity production, the patriarchal division of labor continued but took a slightly different form. As Jensen (1980) notes, most male farmers abandoned the philosophy of self-sufficiency long before farm women. Women's work on the farm often involved the production of goods and services for use, while men produced goods primarily for the market.

A strong interdependence of women and men continues to exist on farms today. The family farm is upheld as the natural and ideal means of producing agricultural goods. Organizing labor through the household stands in distinction to capitalist relations in the work place. Through focusing solely on the mode of production, recent political economy theorists have given scant attention to sexual and racial exploitation in U.S. agricultural production. Theorists, who are concerned with the structure of agriculture, have not examined the patriarchal work arrangements on the family farm.

4

Women Farmers

Introduction

Women farmers are usually overlooked or invisible in studies of farming in the United States. According to census figures, there were 128,170 women farmers and farm managers (5 percent of all farmers) in the United States in 1978. A nationwide telephone USDA survey of 2,509 farm women found that 55 percent of the women considered themselves main operators (Jones and Rosenfeld, 1981), suggesting that the census of Agriculture estimate undercounts the number of women farmers.

A few recent studies have explored women's work on farms (Pearson, 1979; Boulding, 1980; Fassinger and Schwartz-weller, 1980). These studies focus generally on women who live on farms rather than specifically on women who are farmers. Boulding suggests that "farm wives and women farmers may be seen on a continuum with the housewife who happens to live on a farm but is not involved with it at all at one end, and the never married woman farmer who lives for her farm at the other end" (1980:277). Little information is available on the lives of women at the "woman farmer" end of the continuum. As Boulding mentions, the patriarchal system probably pushes women into domestic rather than farm work. Little research has focused on farm as well as domestic work. Through focusing on women who *are* involved in agricultural production, this study provides a description of an aspect of women's work that has rarely been acknowledged.

Pearson (1979) suggests the need for research on how women's production roles vary in different geographical and technological settings. To this end, the Farm Women's Project of USDA recently completed its survey of 2,509 farm women. It examines the characteristics of farm women and their relationships to farm business and work. Although it provides an overall picture of farm women in the United States, there remains a lack of research that investigates the experiences, conditions, and problems that farm women encounter in their everyday lives.

BEGINNING THE RESEARCH

Because little information is available on women farmers, this study is exploratory in nature. Its purpose is to comprehend the experiences, conditions, and problems these women encounter. To this end, I conducted a series of indepth interviews with twenty-one women farmers in Kentucky, Ohio, and Indiana. The farmers in Kentucky relied primarily on tobacco and cattle as cash products; those in Ohio and Indiana relied on grain.

A system of referrals was utilized to identify women farmers. County extension agents identified women who had major responsibility in a farming operation. The degree of the extension agents' help varied from county to county— several county agents could think of only two names. Another agent invited me to his office and went through his files, giving me about fifteen names complete with a description of each woman. One agent set up appointments and drove me to the farms of several women. I also obtained referrals from the women to whom the extension agents sent me, and from other local people. In addition to the formal interviews, I participated in several discussion groups with women farmers and women interested in farming.

This research is not concerned with statistical sampling, which, as Glaser and Strauss note, is undertaken "to obtain accurate evidence on distributions of people among categories to be used in descriptions or verifications" (1967:62). Rather, the type of sampling I utilized here is closer to Glaser and Strauss's theoretical sampling, which they describe as an attempt "to discover categories and their properties and to suggest the interrelationships into a theory" (1967:62). Theoretical sampling was used in this instance to discover women who were farming and to begin to uncover the various categories and properties that could be used to describe them.

In her excellent study of tenant farm women in the South in the 1930s, Hagood explained her motivations for utilizing case studies: "We have tried to adapt the case study method to amplify and to give substance and meaning to statistical descriptions. We have tried to utilize case material to afford a richer sort of description than quantitative measures can give and yet avoid the superficial, stereotyped, sentimental 'case study'" (1977:228–229). Her book unquestionably provides a rich description of the farm women's lives. Similar motives lie behind the methodological approach of the present study.

In an attempt to study another marginal group in agricultural production, blacks in American agriculture, Brown and Larson (1979) began with case studies of successful black farmers. They emphasized that successful black farmers are usually overlooked or concealed by data that accentuates the disappearance of black-operated farms. In order to examine the factors that have facilitated or inhibited blacks' participation in agricultural production, Brown and Larson noted the importance of in-depth interviews of the anomolous cases (that is, successful farmers). The methodological strategy they utilized is extended to my study of women farmers, who are also marginal and subordinate in relation to agricultural production.

INTERVIEW PROCEDURE

Once I had the names of women farmers, I telephoned them, explained to them briefly the nature of my study, and set up appointments. Of all the women I called, only one refused to be interviewed in person (although she was willing to talk with me over the phone). All the other interviews were conducted at the respondents' homes. In every case I had at least some time alone with the women, but often other people were present for part of the interview. During three of the interviews, a son of the woman was present until it became clear that I was actually interested in talking to the woman. As would be expected, the women were more candid when alone. The tone of the interview changed when family or neighbors left.

Usually the interview began in the house, either in the kitchen or living room. The majority of interviews were taped, and notes were always taken. The women were assured that their names would not be used in the study. An interview schedule (Appendix A) was used as a guideline for discussion, but an attempt was made to create an informal interview situation so that respondents would feel free to discuss anything about farming they considered important. I told each respondent that I would ask some questions, but that primarily I just wanted her to talk about her experiences with farming. The interviews varied in the degree of formality and level of openness. Rarely did I go through the interview schedule question by question. Often, I asked a question when there was a lull in the conversation or to bring the discussion back to the topic of farming. Interviews lasted from one and a half to three hours. After we talked inside, I usually asked the women if she would show me around the farm. Sometimes I was shown the inside of their homes, others showed me the yard and garden, while others walked the farm with me, working at odds and ends along the way. Still others took me into barns, and some drove me around the farm. During this time, I took no notes and did not use the tape recorder. Often the women shared more personal experiences during this time. After the completion of the

Table 4.1   Demographic Characteristics of Women Farmers: Age, Education, Marital Status, and Number of Children

Demographic characteristic	Number of women
Age	
25–34	5
35–44	3
45–54	4
55–64	4
65+	5
Education: Years of school completed	
K–8	2
9–11	3
High school	8
Some college	3
College graduate	3
Graduate school	2
Marital status	
Single	6
Married	9
Widowed	6
Number of children	
0	6
1	2
2	4
3	7
4	2

interview, I made notes on the unrecorded conversation and on general impressions. Several times, I helped the women with their work. In one instance I stripped tobacco, and another time I fed cows and shoveled manure.

Who They Are

The ages of the women farmers ranged from 34 to 74 (see Table 4.1). The women were at varying points in their life cycles. Some were attempting to raise families, others were through with child rearing, while others plan never to have children.

Table 4.2   Characteristics of Farms

Characteristic	Number of farms
Number of acres	
−50	3
50–100	4
101–300	10
301–500	1
501–1000	3
Tenancy	
Full owners	15
Part owners	4
Full tenants	2

The modal educational level of the women in the sample was high school. Eight of the women attended at least some college, while five women never completed high school. Of the women interviewed, nine were married, six were single, and six were widowed. The marital status of women is important in determining the nature of their involvement in the farm operation. All of the married women and women who had previously been married had at least one child. The modal number of children was three, with a maximum of four children.

The majority of the women lived on farms that they or their family owned (Table 4.2). Four of the women owned land and rented additional land that they farmed. Only two of the women in the sample were in families which did not own land; both of these were married to men farmers. (Women who are sole operators are more likely to own their land than are men operators. In 1978, 79 percent of women operators owned all of their land, compared to 58 percent of male operators [Kalbacher, 1982].)

In order to explain the nature of the work of women farmers, a typology was created to simplify the diverse situations under which women farm. A number of factors may affect the type of work women perform on farms, including the type of farm, size of farm, race, class, off-farm employment, and a woman's relationship to men. The women in the present study were all white; the majority worked on farms where family labor was prevalent. None was employed as a paid agricultural laborer; therefore, differences by race or between unpaid workers and paid workers will not be explored.

In the interviews it became apparent that a woman's relationship with men on farms was a primary condition influencing her involvement in the farming operation. In her study of women's work on farms in Colorado, Pearson (1979) created a typology of women's work in agriculture. She delineated four types of relationships that women who are married to farmers assume toward agricultural production: independent producers, agricultural partners, agricultural helpers, and homemakers. In the Colorado county she studied, Pearson found that the majority of women were helpers. She characterizes a farm helper as a woman who helps with agricultural production during the peak times of the year. While Pearson's categories are helpful in delineating the different types of women's involvement in farming, she fails to explicitly address the issue of the power differential between the sexes. In order to explore the power differential between the sexes, this study focuses on women who are independent producers in terms of Pearson's categories. Women who are agricultural partners were also interviewed to gain an understanding of the differences in women's work on the farm with and without the presence of a husband. Through focusing on the constraints these women face, an attempt is made to comprehend how the hierarchical relation between men and women affects women's work on farms.

If a woman is married to a man who is a farmer, the hierarchical sexual division of labor usually operates to the extent that the man is a manager or manager/worker and the woman is a worker. Pearson noted that the women most active in agricultural production are widowed, single, or relieved of their housekeeping or child-rearing responsibilities. In the present study, the women most active in agricultural production were similar to those described by Pearson. In addition to these categories, women living on farms who are married but whose husbands were never farmers are often very active in agricultural production. In the present study, women in this situation have usually inherited land that they want to retain.

The position of women on a farm cannot be understood without considering male domination in society and in the family. As has been discussed previously, most women are taught and socialized to view their work in the home as their most important work. Whether or not women engage in field work, they are still expected to have the major responsibility for child rearing, food preparation, laundry, and general housework. Thus, a woman who participates in farm work is in a situation similar to a nonfarm woman who works outside the home. Studies of employed married women have revealed that regardless of the employment of these women, their husbands do not do household work (Meissner et al., 1975). A woman who works in the fields is increasing her labor requirements. In general, women do not independently choose the degree of their involvement in agricultural production.

The family farm is frequently characterized as a work place in which ownership, management, and labor are not separated. The typical notion of a farmer is a man who owns, manages, and works on the farm. While it has previously been shown that ownership, management, and work are more likely to be separated on today's farms, many men farmers do own, manage, and work their farms. When examining the position of women in terms of ownership, management, and labor on the farm, the changing trends in the structure of agriculture are important. But, in addition, it must be recognized that women in America only rarely own, manage, and work their farms. A major factor limiting women's involvement in agriculture appears to be the patriarchal nature of the family farm. When women live on farms with men, the men usually exercise control of the farm operation. In fact, even when women own farms, they often transfer the authority of running

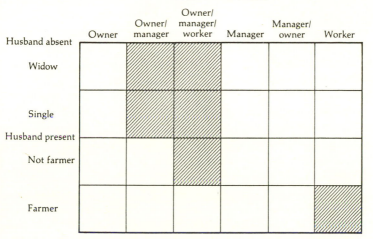

Women's Involvement

Note: Shaded boxes indicate cells into which women in the sample were categorized.

Figure 4.1 Typology of Women's Work on Farms.

the farm enterprise to their husbands (Salamon and Keim, 1979).

In constructing a typology of women's ownership, management, and labor on farms, the major variable used is the woman's relationships to men on the farm. Figure 4.1 shows the relationship between this factor and their position in the ownership, management, and labor on the farm. The shaded boxes indicate the cells into which the women in the sample were categorized. The four categories of women's relationships to men on farms are widows, single women, women married to men who are not farmers, and women married to men who are farmers.

A discussion of these four categories, with two case studies from each category, follows. The names of the women have been changed to protect their privacy.

WIDOWS

Widowhood is the time in the life cycle of farm women when they generally exercise the most power (Salamon and

Keim, 1979). With the death of their husbands, many farm women take over ownership and management of the farm operation. Until 1981, inheritance tax laws discriminated against farm women to the extent that they often lost their farms. Landownership gives women more power. Due to the inheritance laws, women who have inherited land from their families have been more likely to be able to retain the farm after their husbands' deaths. The widows in this study who inherited land from their parents were more involved in the farm operation than women who inherited land only after the deaths of their husbands.

The extent of women's lifetime involvement in the farm operation was a conditioning factor in how they experienced their lives as farmers. The majority of widows interviewed had been farmers prior to their husbands' deaths, while others had been only minimally involved in the farm operation when their husbands were alive. Three of the four women who farmed while their husbands were alive were married to men who had not been farmers. These three women had inherited land from their families, and their husbands had never been interested in farming. All four of the women who were farmers prior to becoming widows prefer outside work to inside work. Each of their farms specializes in cattle, corn, and tobacco. These women have all been quite involved in farm labor. The woman on the largest, most prosperous farm has been involved in the least amount of actual farm labor. Although she points out that she has been in the field with the men, she knows "other women who have done just as hard of work as a man ever has." In fact, the three other women who were farmers prior to their husbands' deaths have performed all the work that men generally perform on the farm. These women have all driven tractors, taken care of livestock, worked with tobacco, and done repair work on their farms. Each commented that male farmers have the advantage of being physically stronger than women. But at the same time, each woman felt she could keep up fairly well with men of the same age.

Several of the widows had only been minimally involved in the farming operation prior to the illness or death of their husbands. These women experienced the most difficulty in managing and operating their farms. Most of their lives were spent doing work inside the house, but when their husbands died or became ill, they became responsible for the operation of the farm. Bea Gordon illustrates this situation.

Another woman, who was left with a 530-acre farm, had not been involved with the farm prior to her husband's death. She feels unsure about her abilities as a farmer. She describes her situation as follows:

> I really was just left. I didn't know a thing about farming and I tried to learn. I'm learning the hard way but so far I've done all right. Farming gives you a feeling of satisfaction even though I've never done anything like it. Before my husband died, I was a housewife, that's all I did, that was my job. Then I had so much more time to spend in the house than I do now. I really enjoy keeping house more than being on the farm. Maybe if I had gotten started with this farming early in life I would have enjoyed it more, but I didn't. My mother was quite a homemaker. She did it all the time and I was brought up that way. Daddy didn't think women should have to work outside.

The influence of men in defining women's work on the farm is quite apparent in the situation of widows. Often the husband's death is the factor that transforms women from unpaid agricultural laborers or homemakers into farmers. Many women living on farms where their husbands were farming have always performed farm tasks, but they have not had experience in managing the farm as a business.

Ability to make the transition from worker to manager varied according to the extent of her lifetime involvement in the farm enterprise. But in all cases, the women seemed quite capable of owning and managing the farm and of performing agricultural labor. Their previous lack of involvement in managing the farm was due to the presence of their husbands and the hierarchical sexual division of labor.

Bea Gordon

Bea Gordon lives on a ninety-two-acre farm approximately thirty miles from a city with a population of two hundred thousand. The property is on a back road about eight miles from the closest town. The land is so hilly that only about twenty-five to thirty acres can be cultivated. The large, two-story wood-frame house is freshly painted. Bea Gordon came to the door in slacks, a nice blouse, and tennis shoes. Her oldest son was present during the first part of the interview but left after he realized I was interested in talking with his mother. She invited me into her living room, which was immaculate and filled with well-cared-for antiques. Bea took pride in her home and gave me a tour, pointing out furniture that had belonged to her mother. Although her house was neat and clean, she apologized for not being more of a housekeeper.

Bea has lived on this farm for forty-seven years and has spent all of her sixty-five years in the same county. Her husband's parents ran the farm before she and her husband moved here. She moved to the farm as soon as they were married, which was at the end of her sophomore year in high school. Shortly after they were married she had two boys and a girl, who now sometimes help on the farm. Her husband has been dead for four years; he was an invalid for seven years prior to his death. For the past eleven years, Bea has essentially run the farm. She has never been employed off the farm.

At present, she runs a cow-calf operation, which involves breeding cows and raising the calves to sell to feed lots or other farmers. For the cow-calf operation she raises fifteen acres of corn and five acres of hay. In addition, there are four acres of tobacco, which she usually handles but is renting out this year. While her husband was living they had cattle and dairy cows. When they had a dairy herd, she did the milking with her husband. Presently, Bea takes care of the cows, feeding them every day. As she describes, "I'm out there with them. I have a name for each of my cows, I talk to them. They are part of me."

In terms of working with the crops, Bea has always worked with the tobacco beds and in setting the tobacco. She also works in the corn, although she was reticent about her work with the tractor. When asked if she operated the tractor, she said she doesn't drive the tractor—that she "didn't want to learn too much." In other words, she felt as if she had enough to do without driving the tractor. However, later she explained that she does drive the tractor if she has to, but she doesn't drive it as often now as she used to.

She takes the responsibility for the decisions concerning the farm operation, although she discusses the crop with the boys. According to Bea, a major problem for her is her lack of involvement in the business end of farming prior to her husband's death. The hardest thing for her to do on the farm is to make such decisions as where to put the corn and when and where to sell the crops and livestock. With the continual fluctuation in agricultural markets, anxiety over this type of decision is not unusual among farmers. Although she expressed doubts about her ability to make decisions in the absence of her husband, she mentioned that a woman neighbor inspired her self-confidence. The neighbor told her, "You've helped your husband, you've raised the children, you've just done so much more than he ever done."

There is some uneasiness on her part concerning her role as manager of the farm. She emphasizes that the farm is a family operation and that they work together as a family. Compared to other women who are left with farms, she feels lucky to have children who will help her. The oldest son, who lives nearby, helps her almost every day. Her younger son lives out of state but comes home to help when he's needed. The daughter comes every week and helps in the yard, but Bea says her daughter could never be a farmer because she isn't fond of cows. Every day that her son comes, she tells him what they will do that day. She expressed some discomfort with her authority. As she said, "Maybe they don't like it, but they don't say anything. We just go on with it." Later, in discussing her inability to work as hard as she used to, she sighed, "I know I'm a burden to my sons. They must just hate me." Sometimes, especially in the winter, she wonders if she should stay on the farm or move into town. She refrains from discussing her problems with her sons. Immediately after her son left the house during the interview, she explained that she tries not to tell her problems to him. "I get depressed, and I try to keep all of that to myself." However, once she gets outside and begins to work she quickly starts to feel better. As she describes her basic feeling about continuing to run the farm, "I feel a responsibility to carry on. I feel like it's my problem to get all these things done and go on with it. I don't know anything else."

Of all the work on the farm, Bea prefers anything that is outside. She has always been solely responsible for raising the children and doing the housework. The garden has also been her responsibility. At least half the food she eats is raised on the farm, including beef. Until several years ago she also raised chickens and sold milk. As she describes women's contribution to subsistence on the farm, "If the woman didn't put food up, you couldn't make it."

Although Bea was raised on a farm, she never worked during her childhood. On her parents' farm, help was always hired. Her mother's main job was to put up food and cook for the family and the workers. When Bea started working with her husband, he taught her how to farm. If she has a problem with farming, she doesn't talk to anyone but tries to work it out herself. She rarely talks to her neighbors and feels as if they didn't help her when her husband was sick or after he died. They belonged to the Farm Bureau when her husband was alive, but she doesn't belong anymore.

The cost/price squeeze makes it difficult for her to keep the farm. She is astounded by the difference between the price of meat in the grocery and the price she receives. Also, fertilizer, feed, and fence prices are becoming higher and higher. Regardless of these difficulties, she feels committed to keep the farm for her boys. As she states, "To me, farm life is the best life."

Ann Brooks

Ann Brooks has lived for thirty years on a three hundred-acre farm about ten miles outside a county seat. Her husband's father bought the farm in 1907 and his family has lived there since. About eight years ago, Ann's husband died, and now at fifty-six she farms alone. Her house was in good repair on the outside, but she lived in only two rooms. The other rooms were cluttered with papers and innumerable odds and ends. We talked in the kitchen, which was large and very comfortable. Ann was good-humored and told me many fascinating stories. She had obviously been working outside that day and wore a flannel shirt and slacks.

Ann attended college for three years and quit to marry her husband and move to the farm. The farm is a cow-calf operation, and she grows corn and tobacco. When her husband was alive, the farm had cattle rather than a cow-calf operation. She has changed due to the dictates of the market.

Ann is involved in every aspect of work on the farm. With the cows, she does the feeding and calving. In the fields, she drives the tractor, doing plowing and harvesting. Last year she raised twenty-two thousand pounds of tobacco and was instrumental in every stage of the work. (Two neighbor boys work for her on a regular basis.) She does all the repair work that needs to be done on the farm, including repairs on the house and barn, fixing the machinery, and mending fences. As she says, "If a repair has to be done, I do it. I'm not good at it, pretty amateurish, it takes me a long time."

Management of the farm is in her hands. She decides how many acres of each crop to plant, the type of livestock, and where the products will be sold. Ann reflects in a humorous way on the work she performed when her husband was alive, "My husband used to say he didn't want me to stay inside by myself, but really he had slave labor." Now that she manages the farm, she sees that her work with her husband was like that of a hired hand.

Several male farmers in the neighborhood help her when she has problems with farming. She consults particularly with one man, whom she describes as a very efficient farmer, concerning decisions such as where and when to sell corn. This farmer is helpful to her because he is quite up-to-date on the market. For additional information about farming, she reads farm magazines. Ann showed me several clippings she had recently cut from magazines. She gets in touch with her extension agent when she needs assistance.

The previous winter she had taken an extension class, where the farm wives took picture framing and the men learned about some new farming techniques. She took the farming class and "the fellows laughed me off." During the class she stated that it was her opinion that girls should be learning about farming and then they would be on the other (farming) end. Again, the men in the class, including the extension staff, refused to take her seriously. In order to improve extension for women, she suggests that classes on small motors, building repairs, and veterinary medicine be taught to women. She emphasized that women are never taught these skills, which are needed on the farm.

Ann enjoys any work that is outdoors. Her least favorite work is housekeeping. After working around the house in the morning she usually goes out at 8:30 and returns at dark. Most of the food she eats is grown in her garden. She cans and freezes all of the vegetables that are used throughout the year. Last year she raised one hundred roosters, which she dressed and froze.

Both her children live out of state, but Ann is attempting to keep the farm for them. Her major worry concerns her income. The profit margin is lower and lower as the prices of fertilizer and gas continue to go up. She says that with no other source of income it scares her to think about things going up. Last year her net farm income was only eighteen hundred dollars.

SINGLE WOMEN

Inheritance is one means by which single women may acquire land and capital. Two of the single women in this study were farming land their parents owned. In both cases, one parent was still alive but no longer active in farming.

In addition to the women who inherited land or have been able to acquire land, a number of single women wish to be farmers but have been unable to due to their economic situation. Women's economic power is much less than that of men. In informal discussions with groups of women who wanted to be farmers, several women explained the problem of obtaining credit. One woman noted that the FHA's picture of a farmer is a man and it is extremely difficult for a woman who wants to farm to achieve credibility in order to obtain a loan. There are many single women who want to farm but are economically unable to gain access to land. One woman called herself a farmer without a farm. She had rented a farm but had just recently moved to the city. Someone was caring for her goats, but she still has a chicken in her living room.

One strategy that single women have used and continue to use is to join together to farm. The group of Catholic lay women with whom Margaret Bell worked have a farm in Ohio that is used as a school and conference center. While these women are no longer farming the land, they did farm the land for a number of years.

Recently, in different regions of the country, women are joining together to purchase land (Average, 1980). Through the pooling of resources, a number of land trusts and cooperatives have been established. It remains problematic for them to begin to farm their land, however. Much of the land that women are able to acquire is not prime agricultural land. While the women were able to purchase the land, there is little additional capital to invest in farm equipment. Also, few women have had training as farmers. Most of the women have part-time or full-time jobs in order to support themselves. Thus, there is only a limited amount of time to farm. One group of women state that their goal is to achieve self-sufficiency. These women, perhaps realistically, do not expect to achieve a profit through the sale of agricultural goods. Their vision is to utilize labor-intensive agriculture to achieve self-sufficiency.

Of the five single women interviewed, three had purchased their own farms, while the other two were farming on their parents' farms. Four of the women do all the managing and work on their farms, while one is the manager and has hired an overseer. A major problem for the women who had purchased farms was how to make a successful entry into farming. Pam Thomas's entry into the horse business illustrates this difficulty. While her situation is different from other women farmers as a result of her higher income from farming, there are certain similarities which transcend this economic distinction. Two single women who are farming a 43-acre farm together also experience some exclusion from their neighbors because they are women attempting to farm without men. As one, Shirley, described, "The neighbors would barely talk to us at first, they wouldn't lend us any equipment, but now they pretty much accept us." One man across the street helps them and they help him, "but his wife doesn't like him to come talk to us."

Single women have difficulty in acquiring the land and capital necessary to operate a farm. While the acquisition of land and capital is also difficult for men, the economic inequities between men and women make the problem more difficult for women. The women who have purchased the forty-three-acre farm both work full time off the farm in order to make payments and improvements on their farm. They live in a trailer on the farm and plan to build a house when they save enough money. Eventually, they would like to support themselves completely on the farm, but as yet that remains a dream.

Pam Thomas

Pam Thomas, who is thirty-four years old, runs a forty-six-acre horse farm. Her modern, recently built suburban-type home is full of antiques and expensive furniture. Everything was extremely clean and orderly and the farm appeared to be immaculately kept. Pam was easy to get along with and quite willing to tell her life story. Although she grew up in Manhattan, Pam always wanted to work with horses. In her teenage years she worked at a stable in Manhattan that housed the horses for the hucksters who sold fruit and vegetables. Her grandparents owned a chicken farm in Virginia, which is where she became interested in farming.

Pam bought her first farm with money lent to her by a friend and has been building up her horse business ever since. The first farm was only twenty acres, but she built a barn and fences and sold it for a profit. She worked for airlines while she was running her first farm. Then she bought a larger farm, which she also sold. Her first two farms were in Virginia, and from there she bought her current farm in Kentucky, which is the center of the horse business. As she explains, "I started out on a shoestring and I couldn't afford to buy well-bred mares." Now she buys mares that are twenty years old but have had good foals. She can buy these mares for "practically nothing" because the big farms do not want to handle them since they have so much trouble getting them into foal. Emphasizing quality rather than quantity, Pam keeps only a limited number of mares; at present, she has eleven.

At thirty-four, Pam works and manages the farm by herself. An older man who is a friend of hers helps her around the farm once or twice a week. He enjoys the work and does not accept pay. She describes her work on the farm:

> In the summer there is mowing, running the bushhog, mucking out the stalls, and giving medication. One mare gets thyroid pills every day. I put the pills in a dish with baby cereal, peanut butter, and karo syrup and feed it to her in a tube. I have to turn them out in the morning, bring them in at night, groom the horses and repair fences.

The busiest time of year is the breeding season. The mares must be watched all night. Pam also rents eighteen acres of land where she raises hay that she mows; she hires help for baling. She has achieved financial success in a business that is quite competitive.

Learning to farm is something she did on her own. She discusses her success at farming:

> I have a firm belief you can do anything you want to do. All you have to do is be observant and watch other people, see what they do and follow. If you go to a big formal dinner, you just watch and see what fork everybody else picks up. People just make it seem more glorious and more important than it really is. Anybody can do it if they were so inclined.

As a woman in the horse business, Pam feels she receives equal treatment from farm managers. Traditionally, many women have been kept out of breeding sheds. Only one farm manager has ever given her any trouble about entering the breeding shed, however. Most of the managers have actually gone out of their way to be pleasant. For several years, she has been attempting to join the Farm Managers Club but has been told women are not allowed to join. Initially, she was told that if she applied her application would be thrown in the trash can. Pam applied anyway, explaining to me she wasn't a "bra burner," but she has to "get along." Now she is waiting to see what happens with her application.

One man in the horse business has been quite helpful to her when she encounters difficulties. He has assisted her in buying mares and advised her in terms of the business end of her operation. In addition, she has a neighbor woman farmer whom she sees almost every day. They often discuss their farming operations.

The horse industry is competitive and tends to be dominated by upper-class families. Although Pam feels accepted by the farm managers, she feels excluded from the social network of horse-farm owners. "Being single and a woman, you are not that much in demand. If I was single and a good-looking man, all the older ladies would be calling all the time trying to get me to their cocktail parties."

Although she is excluded from horse-farm social participation because she is a single woman, Pam would rather farm than do anything else. She enjoys physical labor and being her own boss. As she explains, "I don't work very well with other people telling me what to do. I enjoy doing things with my hands. There really isn't anything else I would want to do. I wouldn't want to move back to the city again."

Margaret Bell

Margaret Bell is farming on a part-time basis at present. She has an interesting biography in terms of her involvement in

farming. Raised on a farm in Minnesota, she recently purchased a 160-acre farm with her brother and sister-in-law
in Wisconsin. On her Wisconsin farm, she has renovated the
house and planted three thousand pine trees. She does not
live on the farm but raises a garden there, which she tends
on weekends. She was included in the sample because of
the particular interest of her work in agriculture at Grailville,
Ohio.

The Grail is an organization of lay women in the Catholic
church who work on a variety of social issues. In Ohio, a
group of women in the Grail live and work on a farm.
Currently, they hold workshops on various issues and teach
other women who come to the Grail. Margaret went to work
in agriculture at Grailville in the early 1950s. She explained
that there was a back-to-the-land movement in the 1940s,
but many people gave up their efforts when they discovered
they could not support their families. With a woman named
Pat, Margaret was responsible for the majority of agricultural
work on the three hundred-acre farm for eight years. There
was a commitment to teaching agriculture to women. In their
work, they attempted to make the farm self-sufficient. Students
were available to them every week to help with the work.
They planted one thousand tomato plants and about five
hundred cabbage plants every year with the help of students.
As Margaret explained, they had to be quite organized about
what work needed to be done. For example, twenty or thirty
students would come for the planting. "There would be five
women on every row. One would dig the holes, the next
would put manure in the holes, the next would water, one
would drop the plant, and the next would plant. We could
plant in no time at all."

They had corn, hay, beef cattle, and a dairy herd. She
and Pat did all the work in planting and harvesting the corn.
Usually they had seventy-five beef cattle and sixty-five dairy
cows. Some of the students learned how to milk, but most
of the milking was performed by Margaret and Pat. "The
men farmers in the neighboring area used to joke that Pat
and I would milk faster than four or five men."

Margaret's parents taught her to farm. As a child, she

drove a mule team, tractors, and farm trucks. At Grailville, she and Pat frequently tried new farming techniques. They raised their garden with organic methods, often attempting experiments to improve their products. For example, they raised corn and beans together and constructed hothouses where they raised their plants. About ten years ago, the women at Grailville stopped farming because most of the women who came were not interested in agriculture. The land is now farmed by a tenant farmer.

Margaret believes that women can do any work on a farm. As she describes, "We were the workhorses. Women can be strong. I lifted 120-pound bags of wheat and threw them over my head. Women just have to build up to it." She remembers her work on the farm as a most enjoyable time in her life.

WOMEN MARRIED TO FARMERS

As Pearson (1979) points out, the majority of women who are married to farmers consider themselves agricultural helpers. The traditional sexual division of labor on the farm is such that women view their primary responsibility as domestic, while men have the final responsibility for the farm. The married women in the present study were selected because they differed from the women on farms where this traditional sexual division was adhered to. They were recommended by extension agents and neighbors because they were seen to be quite involved in farming.

The hierarchical sexual division of labor often relegates women married to farmers to the role of agricultural helper. On farms where a man is involved in farming, the man usually views himself as the farmer. Depending upon the class situation of the farmer, he is either the manager or the manager/worker. In all but one case in this study, the women considered themselves helpers. In essence, "agricultural helper" is actually another term for "unpaid agricultural worker." The woman who works on the farm with her husband is often in the position of doing what her husband tells her to do. Regardless of whether women work "right alongside" their husbands, they are often considered "helpers" rather than "farmers." As Salamon and Keim explain, "Women work in the fields and operate farm equipment but, like hired labor, are subject to direction by their husbands who are considered the actual farmers" (1979:115). The distinction between farmer and helper is actually the distinction between manager and worker.

Marian Wolfe

Marian Wolfe lives on a farm that her family rents in a grain-producing area of Indiana. Both she and her husband are thirty-nine years old; they have a teenaged boy and girl who both live at home. The small one-story wooden house in which they live is located on their 220-acre rented farm. They own 77 acres of land a few miles north of their home. In addition, they farm 700 acres on eleven other farms which are all within a fifteen-mile radius of their home. Our interview began in the living room where her husband and son were watching a football game. After her daughter finished cleaning up after dinner, we moved into the kitchen. Marian apologized for her house. While she talked, she folded socks, her daughter was in the kitchen doing laundry, and her son asked her to sew up his overalls. Her husband, Tom, left for an hour having told her that he was going into town for a bit.

The family has lived on this farm for fourteen years. Marian was raised in town, about three miles from her present home. She knew nothing about farming until she married and moved to the farm with her husband. When they were first married her husband needed help on the farm, so she began to work. According to Marian, she never decided to farm, she just knew what had to be done. During the early years of their marriage, her husband worked full time in town for eight years. Since it was cheaper to hire a babysitter than a farmhand, Marian worked on the farm. While Tom worked the 4:00 P.M. to 1:00 A.M. shift, Marian worked in the fields at night. At that time, the children were only two and four years old, and she remarked that it was nice to get out of the house. However, while she was farming and Tom was working in town, the other farmers made fun of him. They were farming between three hundred and four hundred acres at that time. Now that her son Tommy is old enough to drive a tractor, they are able to farm more land. Because of the economic situation, they have to rent more land now to keep going, and they cannot afford to buy land.

On the farms they work, the Wolfes raise 550 acres of soybeans, 300 acres of corn, 75 acres of wheat, 10 acres of oats, and 8 acres of alfalfa. In addition, they have a cow-calf operation with twenty cows. They also have feeder calves.

Marian drives the tractor constantly. During the spring and summer, she usually rides the tractor fourteen hours a day. Using their largest tractor, which has a cab, she disks, cultivates, and plows. As she says, "The women do the things that the men don't like to do. Women do the disking, you'll never see a woman doing the planting because the men like to do it."

Marian explains that she has always been somewhat leery of the machinery. "I do as well as they do, but I don't have the confidence." She proudly told a story of a neighbor man who used to sit and watch her drive the tractor. Finally, he told her he liked to watch her because she could drive the tractor as well as a man. Her work on the tractor is not always admired by men in the community. The farmers who teased Tom when they saw his wife driving the tractor while he was working in town are only one example. The previous summer Marian had been "having trouble with her insides. The doctor told me that a woman wasn't made to drive a tractor." She had stopped working in the fields that summer but later told me, "I get lonesome staying in the house. Regardless of what the doctor says I'm going out this spring." Rather than believing that women weren't made to ride tractors, Marian told me that "tractors weren't made for women." The steps are too high and the seats are too far from the pedals and levers. Her solution was to make a new seat.

Of all the work on the farm, Marian likes working with the cows and cattle the best. She helps do the feeding. They previously had a larger cattle operation but are now concentrating on grain due to the demands of the market. "I fought getting rid of the cows. I love them. You have to put so much into them, but the babies are so cute. Everybody thinks I'm nuts."

In terms of the management of the farm, Marian explains that her husband and son make the decisions. As she describes, "I am not the farmer, I'm the helper. I wouldn't consider myself to be a farmer, I only help out. I don't make the drastic decisions, but I put in my opinion. My opinion is expected." She does not define herself as a farmer, because her husband and son have the responsibility to support her.

Marian does not talk about farming with people other than her family. Her husband, Tom, is president of the extension board and makes contact with the extension agent when they have a problem with farming. Although Marian knows the extension agent, she never talks to him about farming. She mentioned that the men farmers usually go to the elevator to talk: "It's like a hen party. It's not a place where women congregate, I don't feel comfortable there." While she feels excluded from this network of male farmers, she does not have a network of women farmers. Although she knows of several women around who farm, she is not on visiting terms with them. In talking about why more women are not farming, Marian stated that "there are a lot of men that don't want women out there. And it could be that the women don't want to be out there."

Unlike most women in the study, Marian usually does not raise a garden if she can get out of it. She can't find the time and she doesn't like to work in the garden. She and her daughter do all the housework. No one has taken the time and patience to teach her daughter to do farm work. The work Marian likes least is housework and cooking. At times she resents the load of both farm work and housework. "Sometimes I get discouraged and I yell. If I spend my time working for them fourteen hours a day, I think they should help in the house. Tom has been good about not saying anything when the housework doesn't get done."

Overall, Marian loves her work on the farm. She doesn't like the excessively long hours, sometimes eighteen to twenty hours a day, and gets tired. Despite all of their work, the Wolfes' net income in 1979 was only ten thousand dollars. Money is their main obstacle and often they wonder if they can continue to farm. But their son has always wanted to be a farmer, so they keep doing this for him.

Billie Johnson

Twelve miles outside the county seat of one of the poorest counties in Kentucky is the farm of Billie and Ed Johnson. The state road from the county seat winds through the mountains following the creek. From the state road, Billie's house is two miles down a gravel road past one burnt-out house, one house where someone lives, and a large woods of good-sized timber.

The brick house sits on a hill on the ninety-eight-acre farm that Billie and her husband own. Billie is sixty-five and Ed is seventy-four. There are not many brick houses in the county, especially for low-income people. Billie heard that the government would give loans to build houses for the low-income elderly, but the government man she talked with told her their income was not low enough. According to her story, she argued for a month or two with this man, telling him if she didn't have a low income she didn't know who did. Finally, they received a loan to build the house and they have lived in this new house for two years.

When I arrived, Billie was sewing a blouse. She and her husband both wore flannel shirts, which she had made, and blue jeans. Both were very receptive to me and glad to talk.

Billie had lived on farms all her life. Both she and Ed "grew up poor," mostly as tenants and sometimes as farmhands. She went to a country school off and on but can only remember having one book. She remembers hoeing corn for fourteen to sixteen hours a day in the middle of July and coming home with fifty cents. She and her husband bought this farm in 1942 for fifteen hundred dollars.

In terms of field work, Billie does the same work that her husband does. They have always farmed with a team of mules and have never owned a tractor. Her husband does most of the plowing and planting with the mule team, but she has used the team. In fact, she has done most of the hay mowing with the mules. The use of mule teams in this mountainous county continues to be common because of the steep slope of the land and the lack of capital. Billie prefers outside work to household labor. She says, "I don't care for the house, I do what I have to do." She does most of the indoor work herself, although Ed sometimes helps her get things ready for canning. Most of the food they eat is grown in the garden. For meat, they keep a few pigs. Billie has a milk cow that she speaks of as "my milk cow"; she has always done the milking for her family.

In town she is known as a good cook. As a source of income, she does sewing for other people. In addition, she has always made her family's clothes. She states:

> You name it, I do it. I've mended shoes, quilted, sewn, mowed hay, plant and set tobacco, done carpenter work, done wood carvings, used a chain saw, used a mattock, and harvested ginseng. I've got curiosity. The difference between Ed and I is that I do everything that he does but he can't do everything I do.

Billie is aware of crossing the boundary of the traditional sexual division of labor. In addition to the labor, she also participates in decision making on the farm to a greater extent than the other married women in the sample. When describing her work, she explains that she has "done men's work as well as women's." A woman in town explained to me that Billie will come to town in a flannel shirt and jeans with her hair tucked up and will sit out in the street just like a man. In a tone wavering between respect and disapproval, this woman told me that Billie just did not care what people thought.

The problem for the farmer according to Billie is that "the other fellow sets the prices of produce and machinery. We exist, that's all the farmer ever does." But she loves the farm, nature, and working in the soil. As she says, "It's my whole life."

WOMEN MARRIED TO NONFARMERS

Only one woman who was interviewed currently fits this category, but three of the women who are now widows were married to men who were not farmers. In discussing this category of women farmers, the past histories of these widows are also utilized. All the women interviewed who are or had previously been in this category are at least fifty years old.

These women take sole responsibility for the farm and consider themselves farmers. While they always made the decisions concerning the farm, they were expected to perform the same duties as wives not working in the fields. In two cases in which the husbands were professionals, the women felt privileged that their husbands allowed them to do the farming. Jane Bryant explained that she wanted to move to the farm but her husband wanted to stay in town. She commuted from town to the farm every day and finally after she spent one summer renovating the farm house, he consented to move there. She described her husband's attitude toward her farming:

> He was always very generous with me. He respected the fact that I had to run the farm because he was busy with his work and I had my father and the two boys. He hired help at the house [several days a week] when the children were babies so I could run the farm.

In addition to managing and working on the farm, these women all had child-rearing responsibilities. All the women had their children with them when they did the majority of their chores. Two of the women were able to hire babysitters one or two days a week when their children were babies. But for the most part, farm work was accomplished while the children were present.

The work load of these women is similar to women off farms who combine work outside the home and in the home. As compared to men farmers, these women's work load is much greater. In no case did a woman answer that her husband performed domestic or child-rearing tasks. A man who is a farmer can expect to have his children cared for, his meals cooked, and his house kept in order. Women who are farmers perform those tasks themselves.

Alice Nichols

Alice Nichols lives on a 125-acre farm approximately ten miles outside a metropolitan area of 200,000. The entrance to the farm is half a mile down a county-owned gravel lane that is in bad repair. A driveway passes through a large yard filled with large old trees. In the middle of the woods stands a small, unpretentious house. Alice Nichols greeted me at the door and we went to talk beside the fireplace in the family room. Her son came in to join us for part of the interview, alternately reading the paper and listening to our conversation. Alice Nichols was quite energetic and friendly, appearing younger than her sixty-one years.

She was born and has always lived within three miles of her current farm. Three generations of her family have lived here since the 1880s. The land was inherited from her mother and she bought her sisters out. When she was younger her main interest was horses. She attended the major state university and was one of the first women there to receive her B.S. in animal husbandry. After college she married a man who was not a farmer but enjoyed living on a farm. The fact that he was not interested in farming allowed her to run the farm herself. As she says, "I'm the main say so." The control of the farm was in her hands, but her husband's work set the temporal arrangements on the farm. "Since he was a professional man, he thought the farm should revolve around him rather than the farm. So at the time we had a tenant and had meals at six o'clock and it held to a professional schedule which it doesn't do now since Tom has been dead for eleven years."

She felt she had control over the farm as long as she kept her husband happy. "My husband just said, 'You be in the house getting supper by five o'clock.' Often he would say, 'Well, why don't you sell the farm,' if it ran into his schedule. But I don't think he really meant that."

In 1952, she realized that the farm was not large enough

to support both a tenant family and her own, so she began
to do the work herself. At that time, the farm had corn,
tobacco, hogs, and cattle. In 1957 she began raising straw-
berries. That was the same year that her youngest son was
born, and as she recalls, "I almost had my son in the strawberry
patch."

In describing her work on the farm she explains:

> I plowed, harrowed, or did anything that had to be done. I
> mowed, worked with cattle, and planted corn. I cultivate, plant,
> hoe, keep records, and take care of strawberries. I'd never taken
> hold of tobacco because someone has always raised it on shares.
> Since my son has tried to raise tobacco, I've set tobacco and
> done all the work associated with it. Anything that has to be
> done, I've done it.

Alice spends most of her time outside. She likes being
outside better than inside and always figures the house can
wait. Usually she will weed, mow, and do anything that has
to be done outside before coming inside.

Recently, her son who is twenty-three has been working
with her. The fact that her son is working with her causes
some conflict. On the one hand, she feels fortunate to have
a son who is interested in farming. If her son were not
interested she feels she might have to give up farming. On
the other hand, she feels as if her power is being taken
away.

> The whole thing has been my decision until the last several
> years when my son has come on line. Sometimes I feel like
> I'm being relegated [laugh]. I used to be able to mow the place,
> but he's bought a bigger tractor so I don't get to mow anymore.
> I would drive the tractors, but they are always somewhere else.
> I'm being relegated to asparagus, strawberries, peppers, and
> sweet corn.

From her perspective, the major obstacle to her continued
participation in farming is the use of bigger machinery. Her
son is responsible for buying much of this large machinery
and she seems to resent that her smaller machinery has been
sold to pay for the larger machinery. As far as the machinery
end of it she feels as if the farm has outgrown her. She can

handle the tractors but has difficulty hooking the attachments to the tractor and repairing the equipment. Another problem is that her son works on other farms and often the machinery is not available to her. Sometimes she wants to tell her son that it is her machinery. Although she resents her displacement, she does not place all of the blame on her son.

> I realize agriculture is changing and the needs of agriculture are changing. We're going to a grain economy. This section is beginning to find that out and not holding to pasture and cattle as much. This takes bigger machinery. I can't get over the fact how much farming is changing here because of the demand of the world. My son is one of the newer breed.

In her mind her son is only adjusting to the changing demands of the market. She is quite aware that in order to survive, the farmer must be able to switch to the products for which there is a good price. However, it is also clear to her that the inputs may outweigh the outputs. They do not have much money now because they are putting it into machinery.

Women face a different situation on the farm than men. Alice thinks women should have places everywhere, but she also believes "they should shut up yelling about not being men because the most important thing is to take care of children." Her impression of the women's movement is that these women think children are passé. This makes her angry because she did her work and had children at the same time. In fact, her children went to the barns and fields with her. When the children were little she had a babysitter one day a week. "To give myself a little time later on they stayed at a nursery in town one day a week and that gave me a free day." She insists she has always done the things she wanted to do even though she never had a lot of help.

In addition to children, a woman farmer has other work that she must perform in addition to farming.

> A woman has to know many things. If she raises a garden, she has to use it, then she has to come in the kitchen and know how to put it up, more so than a man. [In a low voice] So a woman knows twice as many things as a man.

According to Alice Nichols, a woman can be a good farmer because she knows how to take care of things.

> You've got to have a heart for farming—stout and soft. Your livestock wants to be noticed. You can take care of livestock if you look at it everyday and watch it for a while and see what it's doing. It is live, it needs care. I think a woman can be a good farmer because she has a mother instinct. She may not have the brute force, but she can have the management and the care of it to make it go.

Women do face some obstacles in talking about farming with other farmers.

> One of the things that men have always been able to do is go down to the corner store and sit around and jaw. Where a woman doesn't exactly fit in. When you are outmanned you can't go that route. But if you know someone you can go to them. You can go to your next door neighbor, but always with the thought that you're not making eyes.

Alice Nichols farmed by herself for fifteen years before her son began to take an important role on the farm. She loves her land and her animals. Farm technology which emphasizes the use of chemicals, large machines, and confinement of livestock is not consistent with her ideas of what it means to be a farmer. Through the use of innovative marketing and farming techniques and a willingness to change her farming operation when necessary, Alice has been able to make a success of the farm without compromising her beliefs. Now, as she is getting older, she is surrendering some control of the farm to her son. He is not interested in the labor-intensive farming in which she has been involved. Rather, he is moving toward renting more land, buying larger machinery, and growing grain for the market.

Mabel Scott

In one of the poorer mountain counties in Kentucky, Mabel Scott lives with her husband on a fifty-acre farm. They have lived on this farm for fourteen years and before they moved to this house lived just down the road. In addition to this farm, they own two hundred acres of land on four other farms. Most of the land they own is hilly and not suitable for cultivation. Their home is a two-story white wood house that stands out as large in this poor rural area. The house is well kept, with comfortable furniture. Mabel Scott is sixty-five and her husband is seventy-five.

Mr. Scott, who is retired, was employed as a high school teacher in another county and only came home about once a month. Although she worked as a teacher in the local rural schools for a few years, Mabel also kept up the farm. She explained that her husband was not interested in farming and, since he was usually not home, she took care of everything. They had three children who helped her with the farm.

The major cash crop on the farm has always been tobacco. Working in tobacco has always been Mabel's favorite work. She also raised cattle, hogs, and chickens. Usually they had twenty cows, twenty hogs, and one hundred chickens. She sold enough eggs every week to buy all the groceries. In addition, she raised corn for the cattle and hogs and hay for her horses. She never bought a tractor but did her plowing, disking, and hauling with horses. According to her she is quite adept at handling a team of horses. In working with the hay, she disked, cut, and stacked the hay without a tractor or a baler. As she describes the difference between her work and that of women who are married to farmers,

> I've done more farming and harder work than any other woman in the county. If it took a man's work, I'd do it. Most women work right along with their husbands but under them.

Mabel Scott was taught to farm by her parents and also learned through working with a tenant. When she runs into a problem with farming she usually solves it herself. "No one else knew better than me." Proudly, she noted that the extension service used her farm as an experimental farm. She describes herself as an innovator. Her farm was the first farm in the county to use cover crops. As for livestock, she has raised geese, ducks, turkeys, and goats.

When asked if she preferred to work outside or inside, she replied that, "I'd take outside every time, but I keep my house up." All the housework and child care were her responsibility. During the time when her children were young she never had a babysitter; she took the children out with her. The garden was also her responsibility. She explained that her husband could not do the hoeing and, besides, he wasn't very interested.

How and Why They Farm

The typology of women farmers reveals that the type of work women perform on farms is associated with their relationships with men. In comparing women farmers who are not married to farmers with women who are married to farmers, it is clear that the women who are independent producers have more control over their labor and the farm operation. The fact that women married to farmers frequently define themselves as farm helpers can perhaps best be explained not by the amount of time they spend on farm labor but by the fact that their husbands are the managers and they are the workers.

In attempting to further understand women's lives as farmers, several questions arise: Do they consider themselves farmers? When did they start farming? Who taught them how to farm? Who do they communicate with about farming? And what are the constraints on women farmers?

The work that women perform on the farm includes operating machinery, raising livestock, planting and setting tobacco, disking, planting, milking cows, mowing hay, repairing fences and barns, raising gardens, and driving mule teams. However, when asked if they considered themselves to be farmers, only a few of the women said yes without hesitation. A typical response was "Well [pause], I never thought about that before, but I guess you'd have to say— yes I'm a farmer." Of all the women I spoke with, eighteen eventually said they were farmers or they guessed they were. Three women, all married to farmers, said they were not farmers, but farmer's helpers. They worked as much on the farm and in some cases more than the women who eventually admitted to being farmers.

Even if women are actually doing the farming, they generally have a difficult time defining themselves as farmers. This is because of their perception of a farmer as a man. On farms where a man is involved in farming, he is usually considered to be "the farmer" by himself, his wife, and others. The inability of women to consider themselves farmers aids in maintaining men's control of farm operations. Women's acceptance of men's control is typical of other types of power relations. Subtle forms of ideological control, termed "hegemony" by Gramsci, are often used to sustain power relations (Boggs, 1972). Boggs explains Gramsci's notion of hegemony as in essence a "world view." "Insofar as all ruling classes seek to perpetuate their power, wealth, and status, they strive to universalize their own belief system as part of the 'natural order of things.' To the degree they are successful, people will 'consent' to their own exploitation and misery. Hegemony functions to mystify events, issues, and power relations, induce a sense of fatalism and passivity, and justify various forms of sacrifice and deprivation" (1972:98).

Although Gramsci did not use the concept of hegemony to describe male-female relations, the concept seems useful in attempting to comprehend men's control. Through the hegemonic process, which Gramsci describes, men are able to maintain their positions of power. Force or direct forms of domination may not be necessary. Thus, to the women on farms, it appears "natural" that men are farmers and women are helpers. Women, in fact, often "consent" to their own exploitation.

ENTRY INTO FARMING

When the women were asked why they decided to farm, the most common answer was that they were "brought up on a farm and didn't know anything else." For these women, farming was a way of life and many had never considered doing anything else. Other women chose to farm for reasons such as love for the land, desire to have animals, or interest in learning about agriculture. Three women explained that they were farming in order to keep their farms. In these cases, the women saw themselves as caretakers, holding on to the farm for the sake of family or children. Two of the women were farming primarily because their husbands needed help. Both these women were married to men who were renting land, and they felt as if they had no stake in their work except as helpers for their husbands. One woman stated that she decided to farm because she did not like off-farm work. While few of the reasons are mutually exclusive, there do seem to be several patterns of women's entry into farming.

A major pattern was exemplified by those women who were raised on farms and had never considered an alternative to farming. For them, farming meant retaining the farm. In these cases, the farm had been in their family or their husband's for several generations, and the women felt they were holding on to the land for future generations as well as for previous generations. While only three women said that their *primary* reason for farming was to keep the land, all the women who had inherited land mentioned the desire to keep the land in the family as a major reason for farming. Another group of women explained that they were farming because certain aspects of farming appealed to them. The three women who had purchased land were farming because of their desire to work with animals. Other women were farming because they had married men who were farmers.

The overwhelming majority of the women liked their work. When asked if they preferred inside or outside work, nineteen of the twenty-one women interviewed stated that they would rather be outside. Of the other two women, one said, "I couldn't say I was fond of either, but I wouldn't want to be inside all the time." The other woman who said she preferred inside work had always been a homemaker in a large plantation-type home but became a farmer when her husband died. When asked if she preferred inside or outside work, she responded that she preferred housekeeping although she might have enjoyed farming more if she had been involved earlier in life. When asked what work they liked least, only eleven women replied that there was any work they did not

like. Of these, eight explained that the work they liked least
was housekeeping and cooking. The general feeling of these
women toward housework seemed to be summed up by one
woman who stated, "Housework goes at the bottom."

TRAINING AS FARMERS

As has been noted, few women receive training as farmers.
Even women who are raised on farms are often steered away
from farm work and into domestic work. The majority of
men who are farmers have been taught by their fathers to
farm. The women farmers in this study learned to farm in
a variety of ways. Seven were taught to farm by their parents.
Another seven stated that they were self-taught. As one
woman described, "You just come along." The husbands of
four women taught them how to farm. Two of the women
learned about farming through working with women friends
who were farmers. Only one woman said she learned to
farm from a tenant farmer, but several of the widows mentioned the importance of a tenant to their farming operations.
As one farmer noted, "You learn a lot from tenants. You
learn a lot because that [farming] is their mainstay." Another
woman felt that she might not be able to keep her farm
without her tenant. "I have one man who helps me on the
farm and he's been with me for forty-five years. His name
is Dean and he's my right-hand guy. Really I don't think I
could live here too long without Dean because he does
everything if it needs to be done."

ACCESS TO INFORMATION

In order to be successful, a farmer must have access to new
information. Three major sources of information for farmers
are other farmers, farm magazines, and extension agents.
The women farmers were often excluded from the information
network of men farmers.

Women are excluded from all-male informal gatherings.
Few of the women are in contact with other women farmers.
Twelve of the women reported that they did not know any

Table 4.3   Communication with Others Concerning Problems with Farming

Persons communicated with	Number of respondents
Other farmers	8
No one	7
Relatives	7
Husband	3
Father	2
Mother-in-law	1
Brother	1
Extension agent	3
Veterinarian	2
CPA	1
Banker	1
Lawyer	1

other women farmers. Of the women who knew other women farmers, four talked with them only rarely, two talked often, and three saw each other often. The women who had acquaintances with other women farmers considered these relationships quite important. Although women are not included in a network of male farmers, neither do they have a group of women with whom they can discuss farming. In fact, seven of the women stated that they never talked to anyone about their farming operations (Table 4.3).

While fourteen of the twenty-one women reported that they read farm magazines, there was not much evidence that these magazines were an important source of information for the women. A few said they had found useful information, but most only looked through the magazines when they had time. The most frequently read magazine was *Farm Journal,* followed by *Progressive Farmer.*

Contact with extension agents is also a means of gaining information about farming. Since many of the women were referrals from extension agents, there is a bias in this study toward women who are in contact with extension agents. However, twelve of the women in the sample stated that they did not have contact with extension agents. A number of the women reported that they had worked with the Soil Conservation Service. Every county has at least two extension agents, one for agriculture and one for home demonstration. In all the counties in the state in which the majority of the women lived, the agricultural extension agent is male and the home agent is female. Thus, women farmers must deal with a male expert, while the other farm women receive their information from women agents. When asked if it was different for a woman dealing with male extension agents, the majority of the women replied no. Many of the women who were in contact with extension agents found them helpful. Ann Brooks provides an example of a criticism of the separation between men and women in extension, however.

Another woman related a story of sexual harassment by a soil conservation agent.

> Never was afraid, I always conducted myself like a lady. Men always respected me, never had anybody to go out of the way. The only man was a man who came out to look at the pond, one of the federal men. He got a little smart, so I just sent him on his way. I got the feel he was about to get smart and I said forget it. And he was supposed to be helping me fix the pond.

While the majority of women who deal with government personnel serving farmers are satisfied, several of the women's descriptions of the interactions reveal that the male bias in agricultural extension operates as an obstacle for women farmers.

SUBSISTENCE PRODUCTION

The continued existence of the small farm is partially explained by the ability of the farm household to produce goods for personal consumption. Subsistence production has usually been the work of women on farms. In their gardens, they produce much of the food the family eats. While men concentrate on the production of cash crops, the women grow food crops for home consumption. The work of preservation of food is also performed by women on the farm.

Of the twenty-one women in the sample, all but two raised

a garden. On seventeen of the nineteen farms where there were gardens, women were responsible for raising the garden. Of course, due to the nature of the sample, there were many farms without adult men. In addition to gardens, fifteen of the women also raised chickens, milk cows, hogs, and cattle for home consumption. Women produced almost all the food consumed on eleven of the farms in the sample. The value of this production is frequently overlooked or undercounted because it is production for use rather than for exchange. If women's labor is needed in the men's cash crops, the work in the garden comes second.

The preservation of food from the garden was also performed by women. Canning and freezing of vegetables is a task accomplished by the women. Only one woman mentioned that her husband assumed any responsibility for food preservation. She noted that he sometimes helped her get things ready for canning. The work of producing and preserving food for home consumption is an important contribution to the farm family.

CONSTRAINTS ON WOMEN FARMERS

Women farmers encounter numerous obstacles in their participation in agricultural production. Obstacles that women face include lack of access to land, credit, training, and information. In addition, the use of large machinery and the demands of child-rearing and household responsibilities have constrained women farmers. Men attempting to farm also face numerous obstacles, but the focus in this discussion is on problems specific to women.

Control of land is a major difficulty for women. Compared to men, women have limited economic resources and are at a disadvantage in acquiring land and capital for farming. The inequities in wages and occupations between women and men give women minimal access to money to buy land. In most regions of the country, the acquisition of land is extremely difficult for both men and women. Women, who might attempt to enter farming, are in an economically disadvantaged situation. A primary means of gaining access to land is through inheritance. Until 1981 the inheritance tax laws on farms discriminated against women such that women were often unable to retain the farm after their husband's death. As Jane Threatt (1981) of Rural American Women stated in her testimony to the Special Committee on Aging in the U.S. Senate regarding inheritance estate tax laws:

> The farm widow is discriminated against in present legislation at both the State and Federal levels of government. The Internal Revenue Service, for example, does not recognize a farm wife's contribution unless she has generated income from an outside job for the maintenance of the farm. The IRS does not define a farm wife's labor beyond that of a marital relationship and as such her labor cannot satisfy [the] "contribution clause" of the federal tax code. According to IRS guidelines, a woman must prove she: (1) inherited part of the farm land from a third party, e.g., her parents; (2) held an off-farm job which generated income to pay on the family mortgage; (3) made legally recognizable monetary contributions. While it is true that farm women have usually not made direct financial contributions, they have increased the value of the farm through long hours of physical labor. In fact, most act not only as farm-hands but as accountants, managers, and more.

As a result of political activity by a number of farm women across the country, the inheritance tax laws have been changed so that when the first spouse dies the survivor will not pay federal estate tax (Palmer, 1981).

Even when women do inherit land, they often transfer the power they derive from landownership to men. As Salamon and Keim (1979) point out, women often turn the operation of the farm over to men, undermining their source of power. If women do have the resources to purchase land, they frequently have difficulty gaining access to credit. A woman who recently purchased a farm, attending one of the discussion groups of women farmers, explained her attempt to buy cattle: "I really expected to be treated like a person when I went to the bank to get a loan to buy cattle. The loan officer couldn't even believe that I was a farmer."

Another constraint on women farmers is the increased use of large machinery. While women are able to operate large, heavy machinery, several complained about the difficulty of "hooking up the machinery and working with the hydraulic hoses." Women are rarely trained to use this equipment, and often the machinery is designed to be operated by men. One woman changed the seat on her tractor because she could not reach the pedals. The distance from the seat to the controls is often too long, especially for small women. As men buy more and larger machinery, women are less likely to operate it. According to Sawer's (1973) study of decision making on farms, men had the primary responsibility for deciding whether to buy farm equipment on 64 percent of all farms. The decision about what make of equipment to buy was made primarily by the husband on 96 percent of all the farms. Women are able to use the large machinery, but they may be more likely to see the limitations of it than are men. During an interview in which both the woman and her husband were present, the man was extolling the qualities of his new no-till planter. The woman explained that they did not need to buy such a large piece of equipment and actually a smaller machine would have been better. Another woman was farming with her son who continually was buying larger and larger equipment. She felt there was no sound reason to spend so much money on large equipment.

The use of large, heavy machinery is used as a reason to exclude women from agricultural production. As a case study noted, one woman was told by her doctor that women were not made to drive tractors. Another woman told about driving the tractor by the road when her neighbor drove by; noticing it was a woman on the tractor, he kept staring at her, not watching the road, and ran off into a ditch. The experiences of these women suggest that both direct and indirect pressures keep women off this machinery.

HOUSEHOLD LABOR

Women on farms are responsible for the majority of domestic and child-rearing tasks. Women who are active in farming are adding farm work to their domestic responsibilities—washing, cooking, cleaning, canning, shopping, and child rearing—when they are not working in the fields. Even when women work with men in the fields, men seldom take responsibility for work inside the house. While urban working women experience a similar difficulty in performing labor both in the home and outside the home, farm women are also expected to contribute to the household through food preservation. Household work on a farm therefore requires a type of production that is not commonplace among urban women.

5

Women and Agricultural Development

Agricultural production in the United States is based on men's control of land, cash crops, machinery, and women's labor. As the present study reveals, women have been and continue to be involved in agricultural production in the United States as farmers, wage laborers, unpaid laborers, and subsistence producers, but their work on farms has seldom been acknowledged as an economic contribution. Many studies of women's work on farms have emphasized their supportive rather than their productive role. In addition, federal and state agricultural programs and policies exclude and discriminate against women. Extension programs emphasize the domestic role of women, often ignoring their labor in agriculture. The male bias in the United States system of agricultural production is transferred to Third World countries through development programs.

The primary purpose of agricultural development is to increase agricultural production. Developers assumed that increased food production through the capitalization of agriculture would yield food for local people as well as for profit. The emphasis on production without simultaneous focus on the issues of distribution and equity has often resulted in increased deprivation for the rural poor, however. While all small farmers suffer, women farmers are at a particular disadvantage. A number of studies have revealed that "development" has had adverse consequences for women in Third World countries (Tinker, 1976; Boserup, 1970; Staudt, 1979; Flora, 1978). With development, women's work load increases, the status of women's work decreases, and poor rural women have increased difficulty in meeting the subsistence needs of their families, with the result often being malnutrition. The development process has actually increased the difficulty of many rural women's everyday lives by excluding women from access to modern agricultural techniques.

Women's Agricultural Labor in Developing Countries

The positions of both women and men in developing countries have been defined by relations of economic and political dependency, first on Europe and then the United States, since the beginnings of colonialism in the sixteenth and seventeenth centuries. Contrary to the evolutionary theories of social change which suggest that all societies pass through a number of successive stages of progress and development, Wallerstein (1974) and Gunder Frank (1969) suggest that underdevelopment is not simply a stage a country passes through on its way to becoming a developed country. While Rostow's (1962) work was used as a model for development, it soon became apparent to numerous scholars and policy makers that development did not proceed according to a universal set of stages in all countries. Gunder Frank (1969) stated that the underdeveloped condition of a country that had been in contact with developed countries was not merely a period of transition before it became a developed country but rather the product of contact with developed countries.

Women's work in agriculture in developing countries differs from that in the developed countries. The transfer of agricultural technology from the developed countries to developing countries has altered the sexual division of labor in the developing countries.

In developing countries, women are engaged primarily in subsistence production. Deere (1976) provides an analysis of rural women's work in the periphery. According to her theory, women's work in subsistence agriculture allows the male wage to be lower than is necessary to maintain a family. Women are able to support their families through subsistence activities, therefore plantations and export industries have hired male workers at wage levels that will not support women and children. The low value of labor power then contributes to capital accumulation in the developing country and is transferred to the developed nations through unequal exchange.

The work women perform and their status are defined through an interplay of the indigenous society and patterns of colonization or integration into the world system. In many parts of the world, particularly Africa, women have worked in autonomous spheres in which they maintained control of the products of their labor. Sexual inequality and the sexual division of labor varied in indigenous societies. For example, in ethnic groups where patrilineal descent was prevalent, men had more power, while in societies where matrilineal descent existed, sexual inequality was likely to be reduced. Development programs, which assume that women's work is peripheral, have often failed to see the centrality of women's work in local economies. As Germain (1976–77) points out, developers recognize women as reproducers but ignore them as producers.

The Interplay Between Traditional Sexual Division of Labor and Colonization

Women have and continue to be the primary food producers in many parts of the world. In subsistence societies women contribute a significant portion of the agricultural labor. Often women in traditional societies were subordinate to males. The intrusion of colonizers seldom improved the situation of women. Rather, as E. Reid (1978) points out, the sexism of the new world combines with the sexism of the old world such that women are seldom the beneficiaries of changes instigated by colonial rule. In fact, as Tinker explains, "erosion of the role that women played in subsistence economies began under colonial rule" (1976:25). Colonial policies, which were often aimed at increasing the production of cash crops, favored men. Colonialism involved numerous processes that altered the status of women: the separation between social and domestic labor, large-scale production for the market, and the spread of private property (Mullings, 1976). Many of the policies and processes of colonial rule concentrated on men. "Male hierarchies were used for direct or indirect forms of colonial rule, while female hierarchies atrophied or were actively suppressed, particularly by missionary organizations" (Rogers, 1979:36). According to Rogers, much of the ideology of male dominance was passed from the colonizers to the local educated male elite. As the tribal bonds began to weaken, men attempted to retain their position of authority through western justification, such as education as a substitute for tribal rights (Boserup, 1970). Rogers suggests that the educated males in many cases are more hostile to women than are uneducated men.

Women's control of agricultural production is tied to their access to land. Colonial policies often undermined women's access to land through encouragement of private ownership of land. Women farmers often had users' rights to land rather than actual ownership.

Colonization often involved the disruption of communal land-tenure systems such that ownership of land was passed to individual men. Tinker (1976) notes that this type of colonial policy was utilized by the Chinese in Southeast Asia and the Spanish in Latin America, as well as by the Europeans in Africa and Asia. In Rhodesia, where women had been independent cultivators, European land reforms completed in 1957 allocated land to men and widows but prohibited married women from owning land (Boserup, 1970). Boserup presents an example of the transfer of land rights from women to men in Southeast Asia. In the Negri Sembilan area of Malaya, where women cultivators held land for rice cultivation, the British administration passed laws that only the land under actual cultivation would be passed from mother to daughter. Thus, in this area, where shifting cultivation was the rule, land passed out of female control.

Rogers (1979) also discusses the taking of women's land as a worldwide phenomenon. She mentions that the elimination of women's rights to land is particularly apparent in Africa because land tenure there has been less affected by population pressure and westernization is a more recent phenomenon compared to other places on the globe. Citing several studies in Africa, Rogers explains that colonial administrators frequently confused land allocation rights of traditional male leaders with the concept of private ownership of land, thereby erroneously assuming that all land belonged to men. Traditional systems that guaranteed women's access to land were destroyed. Women continued to farm land but were increasingly dependent on the men who owned the land (Tinker, 1976).

The emphasis of colonial regimes on cash crop production at the expense of subsistence production has been directed toward men. Taxation policies often forced men to take jobs on plantations while women remained in the villages with their children and the subsistence crops (Tinker, 1976). In Asia and some places in Latin America, entire families worked on plantations, but only the man was regarded as the employee and the remainder of the family worked for him. Although these colonial policies exploited the labor of men as well as women, the impact of land reforms and the introduction of cash-crop production often resulted in greater control by the male in the family.

The Interplay Between Agricultural Development and Industrial Development

Prior to examining the impact of agricultural development programs on women and society, the relationship between agriculture and industry in developing countries must be mentioned. Modernization usually involves increasing monetization of local economies. Male workers are needed in the cities as industrial development proceeds. The need for cash is often met by men leaving their local villages to work for wages in cities. Male migration to cities imposes burdens on the women who remain in rural areas. In many cases, men are unable to afford to bring their families to the cities. Women assume a greater amount of agricultural work as the men leave the villages. In discussing the situation of Luo women, Hay (1976) explains that women bear the burden of the transition of the economy in rural areas. Women are forced to adopt labor-saving patterns in subsistence production, since they perform the labor that men previously performed, as well as their own. With the expansion of the industrial sector, agriculture becomes increasingly marginalized as a means of acquiring wealth. As a result, the Luo women in Hay's study no longer exerted themselves to build up surpluses of food. Production went down with reduced labor inputs and the inability of subsistence agriculture to provide needed cash.

Although at one time subsistence agriculture was central to the economies of villages, subsistence agriculture is becoming more and more marginalized. Women in developing countries are marginalized as they continue to perform the bulk of their work in subsistence agriculture.

The exclusion of women from the cash economy tends to lower their position vis-à-vis men. Boserup (1970) concludes that economic development results in the declining status of women and increased dependency on men. In a later work on women and development, Deere (1978) notes that even when women have access to income and occupations, the changes in the wider economy reduce the amount of control that women have, thereby marginalizing their position in the economy. As Pala (1977) insists, wages do not necessarily signify nonoppressive conditions. The majority of women and men in developing countries must exist in economies that are dependent on and exploited by developed countries. While development creates dependence of the economies of developing countries on developed countries, it must be remembered that selective groups benefit from development. The increasing literature on women and development clearly indicates that women as a group have not benefited from development efforts. Several authors have suggested that in examining the impact of development on women, a differentiation between elite and nonelite women must be maintained. Development affects women of differing classes in varying ways. While elite women may gain access to cash, nonelite women may be losing their access to their traditional sources of wealth (Staudt, 1979).

The Green Revolution

The discovery of high yielding varieties (HYV's) of wheat and rice by agricultural scientists offered the promise of the Green Revolution. The International Rice Research Institute (IRRI) in the Philippines and the International Center for the Improvement of Maize and Wheat (CIMMYT) in Mexico, which have both been supported by the Rockefeller and Ford foundations and a number of governments of developed countries were created to transfer a package of agricultural techniques to developing countries. The aim of the Green Revolution was to increase agricultural production. In order to insure the success of the Green Revolution farmers in developing countries needed to adopt an entire package of agricultural techniques. The seeds of the HYV's are hybrids that must be purchased rather than saved from the previous harvest. The performance of HYV's is tied to the use of fertilizers, pesticides, and irrigation. Thus, farmers who adopted this technology became increasingly dependent on purchased inputs.

While the Green Revolution was immediately successful in improving agricultural production in various regions of the world, a number of problems quickly became apparent to those both within and outside the systems that were promoting modern agricultural practices.

While proponents of the Green Revolution assumed that increased agricultural production would result in food for consumption and a surplus that could be sold for profit, this assumption soon proved erroneous. Through focusing on improving agricultural production, the question of food distribution was ignored. Despite the increased levels of production, regional and local food shortages persisted. The modernization of agriculture has tended to work against small-scale and subsistence farmers. Small farmers do not have access to credit and are thus unable to purchase the new seeds, chemicals, and irrigation systems. A report by United Nations Research Institute for Social Development (UNRISD) (1974) notes the following consequences of the use of the new agricultural technology: the concentration of land and capital; regional concentration; the use of labor-saving machinery; the dissolution of rural livelihood; and the reliance on imported goods and world market prices for food supplies. Because they are unable to obtain working capital, small-scale farmers are forced to sell their land, which contributes to the proliferation of large farms. Land and capital become concentrated in the hands of wealthier landowners. The use of the new technology is only feasible in selected regions. Remote areas where access to transportation, water, and markets is limited are unable to use the packages of technology that are being promoted. Therefore, the poorest regions often fall further and further behind the more prosperous agricultural areas. Increased mechanization and the use of labor-saving devices increases rural unemployment. George (1978) explains that reduced employment opportunities cause people to migrate to urban areas, thereby merely displacing poverty from the countryside to the city. As she states, "Large scale mechanization might have made sense in the wide-open spaces of the U.S. where few extra hands were available for farm work, but contributes to social disaster in Asian or Latin American circumstances" (1978:40). Unemployment and the unavailability of land leads to hunger in many countries. In some regions there has also been a decline in the amount of land planted in crops other than wheat and rice, which has resulted in declining nutrition.

The problems associated with the Green Revolution have been acknowledged by many of its proponents. The Green Revolution was conceived for the purposes of expanding the

U.S. agricultural inputs market, providing food for urban people, and creating a stable, prosperous rural bourgeoisie in developing countries (George, 1978). According to George, this last was attempted in order to minimize the need for agrarian reform. Often, however, the policies associated with the Green Revolution have led to increased rural unrest. As a result, international agricultural research centers are instituting programs and technology specifically aimed at small-scale farmers. Several of the centers are emphasizing farming systems as opposed to promoting single commodity farming.

While the majority of small farmers suffer with the introduction of "improved" agricultural technology, women farmers are at a particular disadvantage. Not only are women usually small farmers, but they are also excluded from agricultural development programs. The development policies, which have attempted to increase agricultural production, have often failed. This can be partially explained by their failure to adequately assess the labor contribution of women in developing countries.

Women and Development Planners

Development planners have tended to assume that men are the most productive workers. There has been worldwide failure to evaluate the contribution of women to productive activity (Tinker and Bramsen, 1976). Approaching agricultural development from a Western perspective, planners define the U.S. agricultural system as the ideal. Women's contribution to agricultural production in the United States has remained invisible. Policy makers, operating on the erroneous assumption that women are not active in U.S. agriculture, have attempted to transfer a male-dominated agriculture to other countries. Thus, planners have often assumed that women's activities have no economic value. As Germain (1976–77) points out, women are seen primarily as reproducers and their role as producers ignored by development planners. From the perspective of the planners and policy makers, women's primary economic contribution is the reproduction of the labor force. Therefore, development programs have focused on women as reproducers. Programs for women have been in health, family planning, nutrition, child care and home economics. As Germain (1976–77) observes, these policies are contradictory in the sense that the motherhood role is reinforced at the same time that governments are concerned with population growth.

In subsistence societies, women are quite active in agricultural production and generally perform at least 50 percent of the work (Tinker and Bramsen, 1976). Particularly in African countries, women have often been the primary providers of food, clothing, and shelter for their families. With the modernization of the agricultural sector, women have been excluded from economic opportunity. The exclusion of women from development programs has negative impacts on women's lives, and society in general. For women, the consequences of development include increased work loads, loss of existing employment, changes in the reward structures for their work, and loss of control of land. Since women have often been responsible for meeting the subsistence needs of their families, their exclusion from development programs has resulted in problems of malnutrition in many places. As development programs emphasize the importance of cash crops usually grown by men, subsistence production suffers. Tinker describes this situation:

> In rural areas the move toward cash cropping has had devastating effects on women's ability to feed their families. Study after study shows that the best land goes for cash crops, that too little land is left for women's vegetable gardens, that women therefore lack money to buy food they at one time grew, that nutritional levels of the women and children fall even when the family income rises. [1981:12]

In many developing countries, particularly in Africa, women have primary responsibility for meeting the day-to-day needs of their families. The most pressing problem that women in developing countries face is malnutrition (E. Reid, 1978). As Mead (1976–77) emphasizes, women cannot forget that the primary purpose of raising food is to feed people, since their everyday existence is spent feeding, preserving, processing, and distributing food. As women are removed from participation in decision making concerning food, malnutrition is often the result.

Agriculture for Men

Despite the fact that women are extremely active in agriculture in developing countries, development programs for agriculture have been directed toward men. The model of teaching agriculture to men is similar to the U.S. extension system, which employs male agricultural extension workers to transfer information to male farmers. Agricultural development innovations focus on men; women are identified with the dwindling subsistence sector. Men are taught scientific methods of agricultural production for the production of cash crops, and consequently the productivity of male labor increases while women's productivity remains static. Scott (1980) explains that land that is brought under cultivation for the purpose of growing additional cash crops is often land that women had been farming for subsistence. The best land is transferred to the cash crops, and men. In addition, women are expected to perform labor in the men's fields. As a consequence of women's limited access to land and the demand for their labor in cash-crop production, consumption and nutritional patterns have been altered. In one developing country where the expansion of soybean production for the world market was encouraged by developers, there was a decrease in the growing of peas, the staple protein crop for the poor. The result was a rise in pea prices and an increase in malnutrition, since the poor ate primarily starch rather than their previously balanced diet (Scott, 1980). The relative decline in women's productivity leads to a decline in women's status within agriculture, which in turn leads women to reduce cultivation or perhaps move to town (Boserup, 1970).

A variety of administrative measures "have been applied to promote cash-crop production for export as a male-controlled enterprise in smallholder agriculture" (Rogers, 1979:142). As in the U.S., the factors which have worked against women in agriculture in developing countries include policies relating to extension, mechanization, land, marketing, taxation, credit, inputs, training, and education.

Extension provides farmers with access to information and training. As in the United States, the agricultural extension service in most developing countries is predominantly male and oriented toward the production of cash crops. Several authors have examined extension projects in Kenya, where women do the majority of small-scale farming (S. Abbott, 1975; Staudt, 1979). Farmer training programs were instituted in Kenya as the predominant means of rural development. Evaluations reveal that these programs often create poverty rather than improve general economic prosperity. Extension agents make contact with the "progressive" or richer farmers, with the outcome being that the rich farmers get richer while the other farmers are in a steadily declining economic position. S. Abbott notes several reasons for the orientation of extension programs toward men in a country where women do the farming. First, the consultants are from systems where men are farmers and do farm labor. Second, Kenya developers, who are aware that women are the farmers, have been trained with the ideology of male farming systems. Third, the men who are contacted are termed "progressive" primarily because they have resources. Finally, farms that are run predominantly by women are likely to be defined as less progressive because their husbands have migrated. Thus, in a country where women have traditionally been the farmers, extension programs bypass women. In another study of extension delivery systems in Kenya, Staudt emphasizes the importance of class distinctions in extension services. Her study reveals that elite women farmers had equity in the provision of agricultural services, but nonelite women received even fewer services than the nonelite men. Her findings agree with S. Abbott's suggestion that women do not receive equity in service delivery because of both class and sex.

Mechanization of agricultural production has tended to replace women as agricultural laborers in the developing countries (Mead, 1976). Since mechanization makes agriculture less dependent on physical power, it might be expected that the division of labor between the sexes would become less pronounced with the introduction of modern machinery. But, as both Boserup (1970) and Mead (1976) explain, men tend to monopolize the new equipment while women continue to work with the traditional tools. This is similar to the situation in the United States, where use, repair, and decisions relating to large-scale equipment are considered the realm of men. Mechanization has often meant that, as activities that provided women with petty cash have been taken over by men, women lose the cash income to which they at one time had access (Flora, 1978).

The technologies associated with the Green Revolution have resulted in increased inequities in the population in general and for women in particular. In India, the introduction of high-yielding varieties, irrigation, farm machinery, and chemicals had contributed to women's declining position in agriculture: the percentage of women workers who were cultivators declined from 56 percent in 1961 to 30 percent in 1971. During the same period the percentage of women workers who were agricultural laborers rose from 24 percent to 50 percent (Jacobson, 1976–77).

In her study of women in a Malay village, Strange (1980) found that women have always been involved in agricultural production. Rice, the primary cash crop, involves both men and women. The traditional sexual division of labor in which men repair the embankments and prepare the land while women do the transplanting, harvesting, and weeding continues. However, the men's work is increasingly being performed with tractors rather than hoes or buffalo-drawn plows. Women's work continues to be performed by hand. Strange explains that as mechanical equipment is introduced, men replace women. Rice harvesting has become men's work as new methods are introduced, and rice processing is being transferred from women's work to men's mills. Although Strange is aware that much of the work that women performed is tedious and backbreaking, she warns of the disastrous consequences for women who can no longer earn rice for their families. Surveys in Asia have revealed that men tend to allocate less of their income to food, clothing, and shelter than do women and are more likely to spend income on nonessentials. Thus, the entire family often suffers when women are unable to secure income (Jain, Singh, and Chang, 1980).

The colonial policies of transferring land to men continues. In many developing countries, tenure systems are changing from tribal land rights to private ownership of land. As sales of land increase, women are continually at a disadvantage. Since men are encouraged to raise cash crops, and therefore have access to income, they are in a more favorable position to purchase land.

With independence, land reform programs often continued to work against women even in socialist countries such as Tanzania. In his study of two rural settlement schemes in Tanzania, Brain (1976) discovered that women were worse off in these settlements than previously, when they had their own crops and access to land. Under the new schemes, all rights to land were allocated to the men and proceeds of the land belonged to the men. Women lost their rights to land and independent income, thereby becoming more dependent on their husbands. Boserup (1970) concludes that the ownership of land is likely to transfer from women to men even in societies where women are legally able to inherit land.

In the formal educational system, boys are taught the principles and techniques of modern farming while girls learn subjects such as nutrition, child care, and cooking (Boserup, 1970). The extension sytems that attempt to train adults also teach women domestic science. Rogers (1979) reports that the Economic Commission for Africa states that 50 percent of all nonformal education offered to women is in the realm of domestic science, while agricultural education is offered only rarely despite the predominance of women in agriculture in Africa. The failure to teach women agriculture is not always a mere omission. For example a report on teaching agriculture to women in the Central African Republic stated that young men were afraid that training women in agriculture would lead to the emancipation of women, immorality, or independence from familial authority (Boserup, 1970).

Home Economics for Women

While agricultural development programs focus on men, development projects involving women are frequently in the realm of home economics. The ideological basis for developers' programs is that women's place is in the home. The view of domesticity that is characteristic of home economics in developed countries is transferred to developing countries. Yet an emphasis on women's domestic work is not consistent with the realities of the work the majority of women in developing countries perform. As Rogers describes, the home economics approach

> applies a Western concept of domesticity to Third World women without attempting to understand their work in any other than a domestic context. There is a strong prejudice about what women's work is, and if the reality does not fit that preconceived pattern then a strong element of moral disapproval is introduced. Women it is assumed, should spend more time with their children; should do more washing and cleaning; should learn new recipes and so on. The ideology of Western middle-class "right living" is imposed in the same way as among early 20th century immigrants in the United States. [1979:86]

The version of domesticity that home economists often carry to Third World countries is based on an implicit picture of the household "as father (present), mother, and children, a nice nuclear family" (Chaney, 1980:63). This vision of the household is often inappropriate in the United States, and even more so in countries where men migrate and women are the sole producers in the rural areas.

Within development agencies, there is an emphasis on the "new home economics." Basically, the thrust of this "new home economics" is to analyze the household and home production in the same manner that agricultural production and the farm have been analyzed. Home production is seen as an economic activity that should be included in cost-benefit analysis (Evenson, 1980). However, as Rogers (1979) notes, the content of much of the "new home economics" projects remains housework-based. While this approach is helpful in underscoring the value of women's productive activity in the home, it is damaging to the extent that women's other productive roles remain unnoticed.

International agencies and national development agencies have specifically stated that they are attempting to include women in development. For example, both the United Nations and the U.S. Agency for International Development (USAID) have issued policy statements to that effect. As has been discussed, many of the resultant programs have dealt with women as domestic workers. Rather than being integrated into development programs, a number of projects have been exclusively designated as women's projects. "Women's projects" are usually relegated to the fringe of development activity, receiving fewer funds and being the first to be cut during periods of financial shortages (Rogers, 1979). A number of scholars and policy makers have demanded that women should be integrated into ongoing development projects rather than being relegated to small projects exclusively for women.

The segregation of women's projects has often been accomplished through defining women's interests primarily as domestic. In her report on a project in Jamaica, Chaney (1980) describes the difficulties encountered when working with male development planners and traditional home economists. The project, which was integrated into a large development project, was an attempt to encourage women to raise vegetable gardens. But as she describes somewhat sarcastically, "We gave it a fancy name, however; we called it the Family Food Production Plan. This was to mystify and impress the men a little bit. And also to get the women's component linked back into the main project goal, which is to increase agricultural productivity" (1980:54).

The difficulty of integrating women's projects with larger projects is related to the predominance of home economists in women's development programs. The traditional home economists did not consider gardening their concern and were accustomed to considering food as a "given" (Chaney, 1980). Home economists are on the fringes of development projects. Their discipline is oriented to a "woman only" clientele. Since the number of development projects related to women are few in number, it is understandable why the home economists want control over these projects. But in order for home economists to meet the needs of rural women in developing countries, they must look beyond their Western bias to women's other productive roles. The separation of agricultural extension and home economics extension that is characteristic of the United States' extension system has been transferred to Third World countries. This pattern of sexual segregation encourages the domestication of women in both developed and developing countries.

Some planners have argued that encouraging women to participate in development programs in nondomestic spheres is imposing Western feminism on women in developing countries. But, in fact, development causes changes in sex roles and the family which often infringe on the traditional rights of women. Germain (1976–77) suggests that the inclusion of women in development programs is not Western feminism but an attempt to increase the resource base of societies through reducing poverty.

The exclusion of women from agricultural development projects has had enormous consequences for the entire rural population. Since women are farmers, agricultural workers, and often heads of households in developing countries, programs that do not include women often fail. In many rural areas, agriculture cannot be modernized and productivity cannot be increased unless rural women benefit from agricultural programs (Safilios-Rothschild, 1980). Women in most developing countries are the distributors of food. As their access to income or land diminishes, the women are less able to meet the subsistence needs of their families resulting in malnutrition.

Staudt (1979) points out that women in developing countries may be quite receptive to programs that emphasize domesticity and their familial roles, but these women are often the elite women. Elite women who have had Western-type education have learned that to be domestic is to be "modern." Therefore, the fact that some women in developing countries welcome policies that emphasize that women's proper place is in the home does not mean that all rural women accept or benefit from these policies. The nonelite women are often the ones who are most disadvantaged by many development policies, since such policies often reduce their access to food.

Conclusions and Recommendations

The erroneous assumption that women are not involved in agricultural production in the United States has influenced agricultural development programs throughout the world. The male bias in the U.S. system of agriculture has been transferred to developing countries such that women's power and access to resources in agriculture are lessened. The continual shift to large-scale commercial agriculture throughout the world has excluded women from decision making related to food. As Mead described women's displacement from decisions concerning food in developing countries:

> Over the years, decisions about the allocation of food and marketing, and about the allotment of fertilizers and pesticides for growing subsistence or cash crops were transferred first from the village to the provincial city, then to the capital city and finally to the international marketplace. These decisions thereby increasingly became removed from the daily input of women. [1976:10]

As food production, processing, and distribution continually shift to the level of global transactions, women are excluded. While women's participation in agricultural work relative to that of men seems to be increasing in various sectors of the world economy, their participation is often limited to performing low-skill agricultural tasks. The fact that women contribute labor to agricultural production does not mean they also make decisions. Women's work in agriculture is often for subsistence or on small-scale farms. Throughout the world women are substituting their labor for the work that men previously performed as men are employed off the farm. While there is some indication that women gain more independence through the performance of previously male agricultural tasks, it must be kept in mind that the agricultural sector in which they work is becoming increasingly marginal.

The constraints that limit women from full participation in agricultural decision making vary in different sectors of the world. A major factor throughout the world is the male bias toward women's participation. The male bias operates to such an extent that women's labor contribution to agriculture is not recognized and when recognized is downplayed. Policies that promote commercial agriculture often work against the female farmer. Her lack of access to land, extension, training, and credit all severely hamper her ability to succeed as a farmer. In addition, women are expected to perform domestic work and child rearing. Government policies, which are supported by science, have encouraged the domestication of women throughout the world.

The fact that women have traditionally performed domestic work, which involved the production, processing, and distribution of food, raises some serious questions concerning women's displacement from this work. Women are still expected to perform domestic work, but the nature of this work has altered. In developed countries, women are encouraged to consume rather than produce. In the developing countries, women must produce the subsistence needs of their family as men are drawn away to the urban areas to find employment.

In all regions of the world, women continue to be expected to provide food for men and children whether they produce the food or buy products produced by others. As Mead (1976–77) emphasizes, issues of food have been the concern of women for ages. While the majority of the world's women are responsible for the care of children, the preparation of food, and the distribution of food to their families, they will not forget that the main purpose of food is to nourish human beings. Rather than viewing food primarily as a commodity, women are forced to see the use-value of food. Women will not always act in the interest of other women or for the benefit of the disadvantaged classes, but because of their daily involvement in feeding people they are likely to be aware of the nourishment qualities of food as opposed to its cash value. Removing the control of decisions relating to food from women may have disastrous consequences for the world population.

While this study focused primarily on women who are farmers, a number of other directions for research on women in agriculture emerged. Further research is needed on women in different agricultural classes. Research on women agricultural laborers would provide needed information on women's work in agriculture. In addition, a study of women involved in large-scale corporate agriculture might provide interesting insights into the differences between women and men in positions of authority. As has been discussed, the extent of women's involvement in the farm operation varies by the type of farm. Research that examines the changes in women's work with changes in technology in specific crops would provide a detailed example of the way in which capital-intensive farming has an impact on women's work. An evaluation of how extension serves women would also be of interest. Another aspect of women involved in agriculture which demands further investigation is the cooperation and collective work of women in rural women's organizations.

In order to ensure sound food policies, women must be included at all levels. International organizations and agencies must have women in key positions. Women must not be segregated in programs with little access to resources. The inclusion of women in decisions relating to agriculture at the national and local level must also be undertaken. Women's work in agriculture must be recognized.

Specifically, agricultural extension agents should not be solely males serving other males. The separation of home economics extension from agricultural extension must be reevaluated, especially in developing countries. Policies that determine access to resources such as land, credit, and equipment must be directed toward women as well as men. The division of agricultural science from home economics and nutrition science into spheres for males and females respectively must be restructured. The relegation of females to fields such as nutrition and food science has resulted in these fields being devalued in comparison to agriculture. The interconnection between agricultural production and the consumption and distribution of food could be recognized through the breaking down of the barriers between disciplines.

Women in agriculture have often worked together in either formal or informal organizations. Due to the patriarchal bias that operates in conjunction with the capitalist system in attempting to retain women as a reserve labor force and as reproducers of laborers, women as individuals face numerous constraints in their attempts to make decisions in agricultural production. Rural women's organizations should be supported through governmental and foundation funding for the purpose of empowering women to increase their participation in decisions related to agriculture and food.

Bibliography

Abbott, Edith. 1910. *Women in Industry*. New York: D. Appleton and Company.

Abbott, Susan. 1975. "Women's Importance for Kenyan Rural Development." *Community Development Journal* 10(3):179–82.

Allen, Ruth. 1931. *The Labor of Women in the Production of Cotton*. Austin: University of Texas Press.

Ankarloo, Bengt. 1979. "Agriculture and Women's Work: Directions of Change in the West, 1700–1900." *Journal of Family History* 4(2):111–20.

Average, Salad. 1980. "An Open Letter on Women's Land." *New Women's Times*, February 1–14:9.

Baker, Elizabeth Faulkner. 1964. *Technology and Women's Work*. New York: Columbia University Press.

Barry, Kathleen. 1979. *Female Sexual Slavery*. Englewood Cliffs, N.J.: Prentice-Hall.

Beers, Howard W. 1937. "A Portrait of the Farm Family in Central New York State." *American Sociological Review* 2(5):591–600.

Bernier, Bernard. 1976. "The Penetration of Capitalism in Quebec Agriculture." *Canadian Review of Sociology and Anthropology* 13(4):422–34.

Bildner, Robert. 1974. "Southern Farms: A Vanishing Breed." *Southern Exposure* 2(2/3):72–79.

Billings, Dwight B. 1979. *Planters and the Making of a "New South."* Chapel Hill: North Carolina University Press.

Bloch, Ruth M. 1978. "Untangling the Roots of Modern Sex Roles: A Survey of Four Centuries of Change." *Signs* 4(2):237–52.

Blood, Robert O., Jr. 1958. "The Division of Labor in City and Farm Families." *Journal of Marriage and the Family* 20:170–74.

Bogart, Ernest Ludlow. 1923. *Economic History of American Agriculture.* New York: Longman's, Green and Company.

Boggs, Carl. 1972. "Gramsci's 'Prison Notebooks.' " *Socialist Revolution* 11(September/November):79–118.

Bokemeier, Janet, Verna Keith, and Carolyn Sachs. 1980. "Whatever Happened to Rural Women." Presented at Rural Sociological Society Meetings, Ithaca, N.Y., August.

Boserup, Ester. 1970. *Woman's Role in Economic Development.* New York: St. Martin's Press.

Boulding, Elise. 1980. "The Labor of U.S. Farm Women: A Knowledge Gap." *Sociology of Work and Occupations* 7(3):261–90.

Boxley, Robert F. 1979. "Ownership and Land Use Policy." In *Structure Issues of American Agriculture.* Economics, Statistics, and Cooperatives Service, Agricultural Economics Report 438, 161–68. Washington, D.C.: United States Department of Agriculture.

Boyer, Harriet. 1925. "Home Economics." *The Book of Rural Life.* Chicago: Bellows-Durham.

Brain, James L. 1976. "Less than Second-Class: Women in Rural Settlement Schemes in Tanzania." In *Women in Africa,* eds. Nancy J. Hafkin and Edna G. Bay. Stanford, California: Stanford University Press, 265–82.

Braverman, Harry. 1974. *Labor and Monopoly Capital.* New York: Monthly Review Press.

Breimyer, Harold F. 1962. "The Three Economies of Agriculture." *Journal of Farm Economics* 44(3):679–99.

Brewster, David. 1979. "The Family Farm: A Changing Concept." In *Structure Issues of American Agriculture.* Economics, Statistics, and Cooperatives Service, Agricultural Economics Report 438. Washington, D.C.: United States Department of Agriculture.

Brooks, Sara, and Thordis Simonsen. 1980. "You May Plow Here." *Southern Exposure* 8(3):50–61.

Brown, Minnie Miller. 1976. "Black Women in American Agriculture." *Agricultural History* 50(1):202–12.

Brown, Minnie M., and Olaf F. Larson. 1979. "Successful Black Farmers: Factors in Their Achievement." *Rural Sociology* 44(1):153–75.

Burchinal, Lee G., and Ward W. Bauder. 1965. "Decision Making and Role Patterns among Iowa Farm and Nonfarm Families." *Journal of Marriage and Family* 27:525–30.

Busch, Lawrence, and William B. Lacy. 1981. "Sources of Influence on Problem Choice in the Agricultural Sciences: The 'New Atlantis' Revisited." In *Science and Agricultural Development,* ed. Lawrence Busch, Totowa, N.J.: Allanheld, Osmun.

Buttel, Frederick H. 1980. "The Political Economy of Agriculture in Advanced Industrial Societies." Presented at Canadian Sociology and Anthropology Association Meetings, Montreal, June.

Carter, Harold O., and Warren E. Johnson. 1978. "Some Forces Affecting the Changing Structure, Organization, and Control of American Agriculture." *American Journal of Agricultural Economics* 60:738–48.

Chandler, Irving. 1918. "Farm Women and Food." *Forecast* 16(1):30–35.

Chaney, Elsa. 1980. "The Strategy of a Woman's Component: The II Integrated Rural Development Project in Jamaica." In *Proceedings of Home Economics and Agriculture in Third World Countries*, ed. Miriam Seltzer. St. Paul, Minn.: University of Minnesota.

Cott, Nancy F. 1977. *The Bond of Womanhood*. New Haven: Yale University Press.

Coughenour, C. Milton. 1980. "The Impact of Off-Farm Occupation and Industry on the Size and Scale of Part-time Farms." Presented at Southern Association of Agricultural Scientists, Hot Springs, Ark., February 4–6.

Cramer, Clarence H. 1972. *American Enterprise: Free and Not So Free*. Boston: Little, Brown.

Dahl, Tove Stang, and Annika Snare. 1978. "The Coercion of Privacy." In *Women, Sexuality and Social Control*, eds. Carol Smart and Barry Smart. London: Routledge and Kegan Paul, 8–26.

Daly, Mary. 1978. *GynEcology: The Metaethics of Radical Feminism*. Boston: Beacon Press.

Deere, Carmen Diana. 1976. "Rural Women's Subsistence Production in the Capitalist Periphery." *Review of Radical Political Economy* 8(1):9–15.

Degler, Carl N. 1980. *At Odds: Women and the Family in America from the Revolution to the Present*. New York: Oxford University Press.

de Janvry, Alain. 1980. "Social Differentiation in Agriculture and the Ideology of Neopopulism." In *The Rural Sociology of the Advanced Societies*, eds. Frederick H. Buttel and Howard Newby. Totowa, N.J.: Allanheld, Osmun.

Dublin, Thomas. 1975. "Women, Work and Protest in the Early Lowell Mills: 'The Oppressing Hand of Avarice Would Enslave Us.'" *Labor History* 16(1):99–116.

Ehrenreich, Barbara, and Deirdre English. 1978. *For Her Own Good*. New York: Anchor Press.

Elsinger, Verna. 1931. "The Woman's Sphere." *Rural America* 9(8):5.

Evenson, Robert. 1980. "Note on the New Home Economics." In *Proceedings of Home Economics and Agriculture in Third World Countries*, ed. Miriam Seltzer. St. Paul, Minn.: University of Minnesota.

Ewen, Stuart. 1976. *Captains of Consciousness*. New York: McGraw-Hill.

Faragher, Johnny, and Christine Stansell. 1975. "Women and their Families on the Overland Trail to California and Oregon, 1842–1867." *Feminist Studies* 2(2/3):150–66.

Fassinger, Polly A., and Harry K. Schwartzweller. 1980. "Exploring Women's Work Roles on Family Farms: A Michigan Case Study." Paper presented at Rural Sociological Society Meetings, Ithaca, N.Y., August.

Fite, Gilbert C. 1978. "Corporate Agriculture and the Family Farm." In *Food and Social Policy I, Proceedings of the 1976 Midwestern Food and Social Policy Conference*, eds. Gary H. Koerselman and Kay E. Dull. Ames, Iowa: Iowa State University Press.

Flora, Cornelia Butler. 1978. "Woman and Development: A World Systems Approach." Paper presented at Rural Sociological Society Meetings, San Francisco, August.

Fogel, Robert, and Stanley Engerman. 1974. *Time on the Cross*. New York: St. Martin's Press.

Folbre, Nancy. 1980. "Patriarchy in Colonial New England." *The Review of Radical Political Economics* 12(2):4–13.

Frauendorfer, Sigmund. 1966. "Part-time Farming: A Review of World Literature." *World Agricultural Economics-Rural Sociology Abstracts* 8(1):5–37.

Friedland, William H., Mena Furnari, and Enrico Pugliese. 1980. "The Labor Process and Agriculture." Paper presented at The Working Conference on the Labor Process, Santa Cruz, Calif., March 14–16.

Friedland, William, and Amy Barton. 1975. *Destalking the Wily Tomato*. University of California at Davis, Department of Applied Behavioral Science, Research Monograph Number 15.

Friedland, William, Amy E. Barton, and Robert J. Thomas. 1978. *Manufacturing Green Gold: The Consequences of Lettuce Harvest Mechanization*. Davis, Calif.: California Agricultural Policy Survey, Publication 2.

Friedmann, Harriet. 1978. "World Market, State, and Family Farm: Social Bases of Household Production in the Era of Wage Labor." *Comparative Studies in Society and History* 20(4):545–86.

Fugitt. G. V., A. M. Fuller, H. A. Fuller, R. Gasson, and G. Jones. 1977. *Part-time Farming: Its Nature and Implications*. Ashford, Kent, England: Center for Europe and Agricultural Studies, Wye College, University of London.

Galarza, Ernesto. 1977. *Farm Workers and Agri-business in California, 1947–1960*. South Bend, Ind.: Notre Dame University Press.

Gardiner, Jean. 1975. "Women's Domestic Labor." *New Left Review* 89(1):47–58.

Gates, Paul W. 1960. *The Farmer's Age: Agriculture, 1815–1860*. New York: Harper and Row.

————. 1979, *Public Land Policies*. New York: Arno Press.

Genovese, Eugene D. 1961. *The Political Economy of Slavery*. New York: Pantheon.

————. 1977. *Roll, Jordan, Roll*. New York: Pantheon Books.

George, Susan. 1978. *Feeding the Few: Corporate Control of Food*. Washington, D.C.: Institute for Policy Studies.

Germain, Adrienne. 1976–77. "Poor Rural Women: A Policy Perspective." *Journal of International Affairs* 30(2):161–72.

Gerstein, Ira. 1973. "Domestic Work and Capitalism." *Radical America* 7(4/5):101–28.

Gladwin, Christina H. 1982. "Off-farm Work and Its Effect on Florida Farm Wives' Contribution to the Family Farm." Paper presented at Conference on Rural Women in the United States, Blacksburg, Va., May 3–4.

Glaser, Barney G., and Anselm L. Strauss. 1967. *The Discovery of Grounded Theory*. New York: Aldine.

Goss, Kevin F., Richard D. Rodefeld, and Frederick H. Buttel. 1980. "The Political Economy of Class Structure in United States Agriculture." In *The Rural Sociology of the Advanced Societies*, eds. Frederick H. Buttel and Howard Newby. Totowa, N.J.: Allanheld, Osmun, 83–132.

Gunder Frank, Andre. 1969. *Latin America: Underdevelopment of Revolution*. New York: Monthly Review Press.

Hagood, Margaret Jarman. 1977. *Mothers of the South: Portraiture of the White Tenant Farm Woman*. New York: W.W. Norton.

Hall, Catherine. 1979. "The Early Formation of Victorian Domestic Ideology." In *Fit Work for Women*, ed. Sandra Burman. New York: St. Martin's Press.

Hartmann, Heidi. 1976. "Capitalism, Patriarchy and Job Segregation by Sex." *Signs* 1(3):137–69.

Hay, Margaret Jean. 1976. "Luo Women and Economic Change During the Colonial Period." In *Women in Africa*. eds. Nancy Hafkin and Edna G. Bay. Stanford, Calif.: Stanford University Press, 87–109.

Hedley, Max J. 1976. "Independent Commodity Production and the Dynamics of Tradition." *Canadian Review of Sociology and Anthropology* 13(4):413–21.

Henretta, James A. 1978. "Families and Farms: Mentalite in Pre-Industrial America." *William and Mary Quarterly* 35(1):3–32.

Holmes, George K. 1912a. "Supply of Farm Labor." United States Department of Agriculture, Bureau of Statistics, Bulletin 94, Washington, D.C.: Government Printing Office.

————. 1912b. "Wages of Farm Labor." United States Department of Agriculture, Bureau of Statistics, Bulletin 99, Washington, D.C.: Government Printing Office.

Interrante, Joseph, and Carol Lassar. 1979. "Victims of the Very Songs They Sing: A Critique of Recent Work on Patriarchal Culture and the Social Construction of Gender." *Radical History Review* 20(Spring/Summer):25–40.

Jacobson, Doranne. 1976–77. "Indian Women in Processes of Development." *Journal of International Affairs* 30(3):211–42.

Jaggar, Alison M., and Paula R. Struhl. 1978. *Feminist Frameworks*. New York: McGraw-Hill.

Jain, Devaki, Nalina Singh, and Malini Chang. 1980. "India." In *Women in Asia*, ed. Rounaq Jahan. London: Minority Rights Group Reprint Number 45, 8–10.

Janiewski, Dolores. 1980. "Women and the Making of a Rural Proletariat in the Bright Tobacco Belt, 1880–1930." *Insurgent Sociologist* 10(1):16–26.

Jeffrey, Julie Roy. 1979. *Frontier Women: The Trans-Mississippi West, 1840–1880*. New York: Hill and Lande.

Jensen, Joan M. 1980. "Cloth, Butter and Boarders: Women's Household Production for the Market." *Review of Radical Political Economics* 12(2):14–24.

————. 1981. *With These Hands: Women Working on the Land*. New York: The Feminist Press.

Jones, Calvin, and Rachel A. Rosenfeld. 1981. *American Farm Women: Findings from a National Survey*. Chicago: National Opinion Research Center.

Journal of Home Economics. 1909. "Organization and First Meeting of American Home Economics Association" 1(1):22–39.

Kalbacher, Judith Z. 1982. "Women Farmers in America." Economic Research Service 659, Washington, D.C.: U.S. Department of Agriculture.

Kautsky, Karl. 1976. "Summary of Selected Parts of Kautsky's The Agrarian Question," trans. Jarius Banaji. *Economy and Society* 5(1):2–49.

Kenkel, William F., and Dean K. Hoffman. 1956. "Real and Conceived Roles in Family Decision Making." *Marriage and Family Living* 18(4):311–16.

Lasch, Christopher. 1977. *Haven in a Heartless World: The Family Besieged*. New York: Basic Books.

LeBosquet, Maurice. 1909. "Women's Clubs and the Introduction of Domestic Science into Schools." *Journal of Home Economics* 1(2):178–81.

Loomis, Ralph. 1965. *A Profile of Part-time Farming in the United States*. East Lansing, Mich.: Michigan State University, Department of Agricultural Economics.

Lyson, Thomas A. 1979. "Some Plan to Be Farmers: Career Orientations of Women in American Colleges of Agriculture." *International Journal of Women's Studies* 2(4):311–23.

McConnell, Grant. 1953. *The Decline of Agrarian Democracy*. Berkeley: University of California Press.

Maggard, Sally. 1981. "From Farmers to Miners: The Decline of Agriculture in Eastern Kentucky." *Science and Agricultural Development*, ed. Lawrence Busch. Totowa, N.J.: Allanheld, Osmun.

Mead, Margaret. 1976. "A Comment on the Role of Women in Agriculture." In *Women and World Development*, ed. Irene Tinker and Michele Bo Bramsen. Washington, D.C.: Overseas Development Council.

————. "Women in the International World." *Journal of International Affairs* 30(2):151–60.

Meissner, M., E. W. Humphreys, S. M. Meis, and W. J. Sheu. 1975. "No Exit for Wives: Sexual Division of Labour and the Cumulation of Household Demands." *Canadian Review of Sociology and Anthropology* 12(November):424–39.

Millman, Marcia, and Rosabeth Moss Kanter. 1975. *Another Voice: Feminist Perspectives on Social Life and Social Science*. New York: Anchor Books.

Mullings, Leitha. 1976. "Women and Economic Change in Africa." In *Women in Africa*, ed. Nancy J. Hafkin and Edna G. Bay. Stanford, Calif.: Stanford University Press, 239–64.

Mutch, Robert E. 1977. "Yeoman and Merchant in Pre-Industrial America: Eighteenth Century Massachusetts As a Case Study." *Societas* 7(4):279–302.

Nash, Gary B. 1979. "The Failure of Female Factory Labor in Colonial Boston." *Labor History* 20(2):165–88.

Oppenheimer, Valerie. 1970. *The Female Labor Force in the United States.* Berkeley: University of California Population Monograph Series, No. 5.

Pala, Achola. 1977. "Definitions of Women and Development: An African Perspective." *Signs* 3(1):9–13.

Palmer, Lane. 1981. "How Farmers Led the Tax Revolt." *Farm Journal,* September, 24.

Parsons, Talcott. 1949. "The Structure of the Family." In *The Family: Its Function and Destiny,* ed. Ruth Nanda Anshen. New York: Harper and Row.

Pearson, Jessica. 1979. "Note on Female Farmers." *Rural Sociology* 44(1):189–200.

Penny, Virginia. 1863. *The Employments of Women: A Cyclopaedia of Women's Work.* Boston: Walker, Wise.

Rapp, Rayna. 1978. "Family and Class in Contemporary America: Notes Toward an Understanding of Ideology." *Science and Society* 42(3):278–300.

Reid, Elizabeth. 1978. "Women, Economic Development, and the U.N." *Quest* 4(2):55–70.

Reid, Margaret G. 1934. *Economics of Household Production.* New York: John Wiley and Sons.

Richardson, Lemont K. 1979. "Private Land Claims in Missouri." In *Public Land Policies,* ed. Paul Wallace Gates. New York: Arno Press, 132–39.

Rogers, Barbara. 1979. *The Domestication of Women: Discrimination in Developing Societies.* New York: St. Martin's Press.

Rostow, Walt Whitman. 1962. *The Stages of Economic Growth: A Non-Communist Manifesto.* Cambridge: Cambridge University Press.

Ryan, Dennis P. 1979. "Landholding, Opportunity, and Mobility in Revolutionary New Jersey." *William and Mary Quarterly* 36(4):571–92.

Safilios-Rothschild, Constantina. 1980. "The Role of Women in Modernizing Agricultural Systems: Some Critical Issues," unpublished manuscript.

Salamon, Sonya, and Ann Mackey Keim. 1979. "Land Ownership and Women's Power in a Midwestern Farming Community." *Journal of Marriage and the Family* 41(1):109–19.

Sawer, Barbara J. 1973. "Predictors of the Farm Wife's Involvement in General Management and Adoption Decisions." *Rural Sociology* 38(4):412–25.

Schertz, Lyle P. 1979a. "Farming in the United States." In *Structure Issues of American Agriculture.* Economics, Statistics, and Cooperatives Service, Agricultural Economics Report 438, 24–42. Washington, D.C.: United States Department of Agriculture.

———. 1979b. "A Dramatic Transformation." In *Another Revolution in U.S. Farming,* eds. Lyle P. Schertz and others. Washington, D.C.: U.S. Department of Agriculture, 13–41.

Schlissel, Lillian. 1978. "Mothers and Daughters on the Western Frontier." *Frontiers* 3(2):29–33.

Schob, David E. 1975. *Hired Hands and Plowboys: Farm Labor in the Midwest, 1815–60.* Urbana, Ill.: University of Illinois Press.

Schwartz, Harry. 1945. *Seasonal Farm Labor in the United States.* New York: Columbia University Press.

Scott, Gloria. 1980. "Speaking Notes: Women in Agriculture and Food Production." In *Proceedings of Home Economics and Agriculture in Third World Countries,* ed. Miriam Seltzer. St. Paul, Minn.: Univeristy of Minnesota.

Secombe, Wally. 1973. "The Housewife and Her Labor Under Capitalism." *New Left Review* 83:3–24.

Shannon, Fred A. 1936. "The Homestead Act and the Labor Surplus." *American Historical Review* 41(4):637–51.

Shepperd, Juanita L. 1909. "Home Economics in the University of Minnesota." *Journal of Home Economics* 1(2):150–54.

Smuts, Robert W. 1971. *Women and Work in America.* New York: Schocken Books.

Staudt, Kathleen A. 1979. "Class and Sex in the Politics of Women Farmers." *Journal of Politics* 41(2):492–512.

Stewart, Elinore Pruitt. 1961. *Letters of a Woman Homesteader.* Lincoln: University of Nebraska Press.

Strange, Heather. 1980. "Some Changing Socioeconomic Roles of Village Women in Malaysia." In *Asian Women in Transition,* ed. Sylvia A. Chipp and Justin J. Green. University Park, Pa.: The Pennsylvania State University Press, 123–51.

Strasser, Susan M. 1978. "The Business of Housekeeping: The Ideology of the Household at the Turn of the Twentieth Century." *Insurgent Sociologist* 8(2&3):147–63.

Straus, Murray A. 1958. "The Role of the Wife in the Settlement of the Columbia Basin Project." *Marriage and Family Living* 20(February):59–64.
————. 1960. "Family Role Differentiation and Technological Change in Farming." *Rural Sociology* 25(June):219–28.

Sweet, James A. 1972. "The Employment of Rural Farm Wives." *Rural Sociology* 37(4):553–77.

Talbot, Ross B. 1978. *The Chicken War.* Ames, Iowa: Iowa State University Press.

Thompson, Edgar. 1975. *Plantation Societies, Race Relations and the South: The Regimentation of Populations.* Durham, N.C.: Duke University Press.

Thompson, E. P. 1967. "Time, Work-Discipline and Industrial Capitalism." *Past and Present* 38:56–97.

Threatt, Jane R. 1981. Testimony to the Special Committee on Aging, United States Senate, February 3.

Tinker, Irene. 1976. "The Adverse Impact of Development on Women."

In *Women and World Development*, ed. Irene Tinker and Michele Bo Bramsen. Washington, D.C.: Overseas Development Council.

————. 1981. "Policy Strategies for Women in the 1980's." *Africa Report* 26(2):11–16.

Tinker, Irene, and Michele Bo Bramsen (eds.). 1976. *Women and World Development*. Washington, D.C.: Overseas Development Council.

United Nations Research Institute for Social Development. 1974. *The Social and Economic Implications of the Large-Scale Introduction of New Varieties of Food Grain*. Geneva: United Nations.

United States Bureau of the Census. 1973. *1969 Census of Agriculture*. Washington, D.C.: U.S. Department of Commerce.

United States Bureau of the Census. 1981. *1978 Census of Agriculture*. Washington, D.C.: U.S. Department of Commerce.

United States Bureau of the Census. 1982. *1980 Census of Population and Housing*. Washington, D.C.: U.S. Department of Commerce.

United States Country Life Commission. 1911. *Report of the Commission on Country Life*. New York: Sturgis and Walton.

United States Department of Agriculture. 1972. *Agricultural Statistics*. Washington, D.C.: Government Printing Office.

United States Department of Agriculture. 1979. *Handbook of Agriculture Charts*. Agriculture Handbook No. 561, Washington, D.C.: U.S. Department of Agriculture.

United States Department of Commerce. 1970. *Census of Population*. Washington, D.C.: Government Printing Office.

Vogel, Lise. 1973. "The Earthy Family." *Radical America* 7(4/5):9–50.

Wallerstein, Immanuel. 1974. *The Modern World System*. New York: Academic Press.

Walsh, John. 1975. "U.S. Agribusiness and Agricultural Trends." In *Food: Politics, Economics, Nutrition and Research*, ed. Philip H. Abelson. Washington, D.C.: Association for the Advancement of Science, 29–32.

Weir, Angela, and Elisabeth Wilson. 1973. "Women's Labor, Women's Discontent." *Radical America* 7(4/5):80–94.

Wilkening, Eugene A. 1958. "Joint Decision-Making in Farm Families as a Function of Status and Role." *American Sociological Review* 23(April):187–92.

————. 1981. *Farm Husbands and Wives in Wisconsin: Work Roles, Decision-Making and Satisfactions, 1962 and 1979*. Bulletin R3147. Madison, Wis.: College of Agriculture and Life Sciences, University of Wisconsin.

Wilkening, Eugene A., and Lakshmi K. Bharadwaj. 1967. "Dimensions of Aspirations, Work Roles, and Decision-Making Among Farm Husbands and Wives in Wisconsin." *Journal of Marriage and the Family* 29 (November):703–11.

————. 1968. "Aspirations and Task Involvement as Related to Decision-Making Among Farm Husbands and Wives." *Rural Sociology* 33(1):30–45.

Wilkening, Eugene A., and Denton E. Morrison. 1963. "A Comparison of Husband and Wife Responses Concerning Who Makes Farm and Home Decisions." *Marriage and Family Living* 25(August):319–54.

Williams, Mary E. 1909. "Domestic Science in New York City Schools." *Journal of Home Economics* 1(1):77–80.

Wolfe, Allis Rosenberg. 1976. "Letters of a Lowell Mill Girl and Friends: 1845–1846." *Labor History* 17(1):96–102.

Index